WHAT PRICE GL

What Price Glory?

Helen Morgan

Inter-Varsity Press
Patmos Press

INTER-VARSITY PRESS
39 Bedford Square, London WC1B 3EY

PATMOS PRESS
157 Waterloo Road, London SE1 8XN

© *Helen Morgan & Patmos Press 1967*

First (Patmos Press) Edition, December 1967
Second (joint) Edition, October 1972
Reprinted November 1973

ISBN: 0 85110 365 0

Reproduced photolitho in Great Britain by
J. W. Arrowsmith Ltd. Bristol

WHAT PRICE GLORY?

Preface

WHAT PRICE GLORY? is my own story told beside the story of 'Esther', a girl from the country in which I work. While these stories share the same chapter headings throughout the book, I have not tried to make them exactly parallel, for the stories are too dissimilar to make it possible that certain years in my life correspond to the same years in Esther's. Esther's story is not a true one, in as far as it is not the story of an actual girl whom I have met; but nearly all that I have caused to happen to her has in fact happened at some time to the girls under our care. I venture to think that, in its general pattern, such a story would be typical of a girl in this country, who was determined to resist a childhood wedding. My own story is true except at the end of chapter seven, where, since a character of fact is stated to have met a character of fiction, full truth is not possible.

Some will perhaps be puzzled about the occasional reference in this book to the 'Church'. The country which this book concerns is not a heathen country and there is an ancient unreformed Christian Church within it.

There will be some who will perhaps object to the pseudonym under which I write, as well as to the deliberate concealment of the name of the country which the book concerns. I have done this because in writing by name of developing countries, I do not feel it is fair to draw attention only to that side of their civilisation which they are themselves struggling to improve.

It is my hope that the Christian reader will gain from these two stories deeper understanding of the very different problems involved in following Christ in some countries overseas; and also cease to regard as weighty and unanswerable the problems that meet young Christians at home.

1 · Ready, the Heart

ST MARY'S was a gracious and beautiful church, with its tall grey pillars and carved oak rood-screen. I had not been in it often and I was deeply impressed with the deep-toned organ and the atmosphere of sanctity engendered by the smell of incense and the brightly-coloured windows through which the sun shone fitfully. It was my Confirmation day.

Standing behind Hilary in the aisle, I was tensely watching her veil, for it had been tied on too loosely. The Bishop's hands on her head as she knelt caused it to give up the struggle and subside gently on her shoulders. Flustered, she retired and I took her place, my main thought being thankfulness that my veil had been firmly tied on by the capable hands of the Vicar's wife.

The Bishop's voice was slow and deep: "Defend, O Lord, this thy child with thy heavenly grace, that she may continue thine for ever and daily increase in thy Holy Spirit more and more until she come unto thy everlasting Kingdom."

As I renewed the "solemn promise and vow that was made in my name at my Baptism", I was, as far as I knew, sincere, and my first communion, the following Sunday, was a duly solemn affair. But I had little or no idea of what it all meant, and when, the following year, I found myself and a school-friend travelling up to the Lake District with a crowd of strange, noisy schoolgirls, who were singing some kind of doggerel about the width of the ocean, I saw no connection with that service in St Mary's.

For the first time, that summer of 1950, the Guide company of which I was a member was not going to camp, and my father had happened to mention this to a business acquaintance of his. She had suggested that, instead of the Guide camp, I might attend a Varsities' and Public Schools' camp. None of us had ever heard of these camps, but the title rather appealed to my mother, and so, after a lot of correspondence, the thing was settled and I and a school-friend found ourselves on the 'Windermere Express', one of a crowd of schoolgirls who seemed to be talking a kind of code:

"Where's your veeps badge, Mary?"

"I've stopped using the S.U. in my Q.T."

"Honestly! At that Sissum we had three P.M.s a day!"

"Oh look! There's Mo Harrison and Commy waiting for us!"

When we arrived at the great grey stone houses which housed the camp, we lifted down our heavy cases. A young woman came out of the house with some others.

"Let me carry your case," she said to me and took it from me. I was too surprised to refuse, and met Val's eyes with a puzzled smile. Neither of us was the kind of child to be 'seen and not heard', but certainly we had lived in a world where strange adults expected us to carry cases for them, not the other way about. We were strangers, in the youngest agegroup of the campers, and obviously ignorant.

"Would you like to choose a chorus?" asked a kindly officer one evening, only to be met with blank stares. What was a 'chorus'?

Nevertheless the girls were kind enough, and the first meal went off politely. In the evening, a lady explained the letters 'Q.T.' She said that two bells would be rung and in between these two bells we must be quiet. The time was set apart for those who wanted to read their Bibles and pray. Perhaps realising that the idea was novel to some of us, she said that if we weren't sure what part of the Bible to read, we should read Psalm 121.

That evening, when the bell rang, I looked with embarrassment at Val and then we both found our not-very-used Bibles, which we had been told to bring, and knelt by our beds. It was the first time I had so knelt, since I had said my prayers at my mother's knee. I remember thinking, "Well, I can put up as good a show as anyone else," but I don't remember what I said to God.

In the morning, we were to have joint 'Quiet Times' in groups of about seven. I wasn't so keen on this, and my face must have showed it as I rather sulkily sat on a bed and listened to another adult (now I had learned to call them officers) talking about one of the stories of Jesus.

But the days were fun. I loved the mountain scenery in a way I could not express. I gloried in the long hikes and the games and the happy fellowship. And if, in the evenings, we had to gather in a wooden hut in the garden (nicknamed the 'Ark') to listen to a religious address, well, it was a small price to pay. Then, slowly, the gospel message began to penetrate. "Jesus died to save us from our sin." Yes, I knew that. I had heard it in Sunday School . . . but then I wasn't a particular sinner . . . not a thief or a murderer . . . what had it to do with me? "All our righteousness is as filthy rags."

I climbed Helvellyn, beside me an officer with whom I had several times spoken. We looked down at white swirling mist: I had never seen mist on mountains before, and we watched it slowly drift aside to reveal lakes and hills below.

"But what does it mean," I asked, "that all our righteousness is as filthy rags?"

There came a night when a chorus was taught us, which caught and held my imagination.

Out there among the hills
My Saviour died.
Pierced by those cruel nails,
Was crucified.

Lord Jesus, Thou hast done
All this for me.
Henceforward, I would live
*Only for thee.**

I stared out of the window of the Ark, at the darkening hills of evening. "My Saviour died." My Saviour. *Was* He my Saviour?

Oh, how little I knew. How now-familiar verses caught my attention as new and wonderful: John 14. 6; Matthew 28. 20; John 6. 37. I wrote them carefully down. And then, one evening, came the question asked aloud, "Is He your Saviour? If He is not, will you ask Him to be? Tonight?"

There was a few minutes' pause between the end of the meeting and the evening drink of cocoa. I slipped out and hurried to my bedroom. I did not turn on the light. As I knelt, I suddenly realised Val was coming in behind me. Thinking she would wonder why the light was off, I half rose, but she said quickly, breathlessly, "No. Leave it off. I want it like that too." And she knelt at her bedside.

One more scene and I have done with this glimpse of my Christian babyhood. It was the last evening and the Commandant read from Psalm 22. "My praise shall be of thee in the great congregation: I will pay my vows before them that fear him." She enlarged on this for a few minutes, explaining the importance of witnessing to our Lord in front of others. Then she asked those who wished to offer praise because they had found Jesus for the first time during this fortnight to stand and thus testify to their new-found faith. Scarlet-faced, not looking at anyone, Val and I rose together.

When we were again seated, the Commandant continued to speak:

* CSSM Chorus No. 348 quoted by permission of the author, Nan Millard.

"The Christian life is not an easy one," she said. "There may be loneliness, danger, and discouragements ahead, as well as joy and fellowship with Christ. There will be days when He will not seem to be there at all but remember this: that wherever you are, wherever He may lead you, He has said: 'Behold, I am with you always, even to the end of the world.' "

She asked us to repeat it after her and it was with those words ringing in my ears that I left the camp to start my life as a Christian.

"Behold, I am with you always, even to the end of the world."

*

ST GEORGE's was one of the oldest churches in the town and, like many others, falling into decay. The whitewash was coming off the outside wall in big patches and the stone-work was crumbling away at the top where it met the big thatched roof. However, it was midnight now, and the out-side of the church could hardly be seen: only the lurid paintings within were dimly illuminated by oil lamps and lighted tapers. It was Easter morning.

Esther shrank against her mother as the noise of the drums, the weird chanting, and the thud of the priests' feet on the stone floor in the priestly dance increased in volume. Her hand holding a lighted taper was trembling. Suddenly a curtain was drawn back and the priests in their brilliant robes appeared. They were processing around the church chanting words that now predominated over all. They were words in the ancient language of the Church and Esther did not know what they meant. Every instrument in the church was sounding but Esther was suddenly too tired to care. She had been there for four hours, nearly all the time standing bare-footed on the stone floor. The painting opposite her depicting the devil in an orange hell, gloating over souls in torment, somehow got mixed up with the one of the Virgin Mary interceding for someone's missing hands that was above it. Her taper dropped to the floor and she had presently to be shaken roughly awake to walk home.

She was aware, as she stumbled along the dark stony track after her parents, of movement and bustle in various compounds. Today was one of the biggest feasts of the year. She had spent many hours the day before in helping her mother prepare for the day's visitors. But when she reached home, she could only think of sleep.

It was perhaps a week after the Easter feast, that the conversation took place that was to influence Esther's whole future. She had gone to the water-hole with Tara, her sister, who was six, and quite big enough now, so their mother said, to carry the small water-pot.

"It's so heavy," whimpered Tara, bending forward against the drag.

"But then you're a strong girl," encouraged Esther, gasping, as she lifted the large pot on her own thin back and smiling her thanks as one of the women at the water-hole gave her a hand.

They trotted off along the dusty track made by hundreds of women's feet which led from the water-hole back to the clustered huts of the town. Their mother grumbled at Esther:

"Did you think to take the whole morning?" but smiled at Tara and lifted the little pot down.

"So you are my little woman now?" she said. "And before long we shall be speaking of your wedding gifts as we are of Esther's."

Esther looked up sharply as she was in the act of swinging the water-pot down to the floor, and the moment of inattention meant that she lost her balance and the water-pot fell on its side and lost nearly half its contents before Esther could right it. Her mother flew into one of her sudden rages and, running to her, slapped her hard.

"Why must you be so clumsy?" she cried. "Do you spend half the morning idling at the water-hole just to spill it on the ground? What sort of a wife will you be?"

Both children were silenced. Esther rubbed her arm and started to gather the dead leaves that lay around the hut. Tara moved to help her. Suddenly there was the sound of men's voices from within the hut. Esther started and would have retreated to the side, but at that moment her father and an old man came from the hut's doorway and her father called to her:

"Come here, my child."

Distrustfully, Esther moved forward. She was a child, but moved with the inborn grace of all her people. Her face, though she bent her head before the men, showed promise of future beauty. Her father took her by the arm.

"This is the child," he said. "She will be twelve in the new year."

The old man looked her over, and Esther looked at the ground and shuffled her feet.

"Well, child?" the visitor said at last. "What is your name?"

"Esther, sir," she said, not looking up.

"So you are twelve: old enough to be a bride," he went on. "How like you the thought?"

Esther gasped, and had not her father retained his hard grip on her arm, she would have shrunk back.

"Oh, no, sir!" she cried.

Her father's grip tightened. He shook her, half-playfully.

"Nonsense, girl! You will like it well," he said cheerfully. "What? Not like to dress in finery and ride on a white mule and be a married woman? To have people say you were not wanted and so not wed? Come, come, you are not such a fool."

Esther was afraid of her father but she seemed to forget that now. She stared up at him imploringly, her eyes wild and frightened.

"Oh, please, father, not yet," she said in a low tone. "I do not want to leave home yet."

He looked embarrassed and then annoyed.

"Well, well," he said, not unkindly. "The thought is new. I promise you, you will feel differently later. This man's son is a young man anyone would be proud to call husband. He shall be brought to see you. Your mother and I cannot feed you for ever, you know."

"What country is he from?" Esther asked, faintly.

"The lowlands," was the casual answer, and she was released. The men went on, laughing and talking, arranging the date of the wedding as if the small, black-haired twelve-year-old did not exist. Her mother seemed to have disappeared and Esther stumbled off without being recalled. She slipped through a gap in the brushwood fence and scrambled up a bank. Joseph, the Evangelist's son, was chopping wood. He was a big lad of fourteen, and saw her coming.

"Why, Esther, what's the matter?" he asked, seeing her face.

"I—I am to be married," blurted out Esther, tears rolling down her cheeks, "and g-go into the lowlands." Joseph turned and looked out over the cliff that they lived on. Far below, shimmering in the heat, was the tropical hotland of their country. To descend or ascend the cliff was the work of two days and only to be done in a large company of traders armed against the many perils. If a woman was to be married to a lowlander, it meant she would disappear from the highlands, probably for ever. He laid the axe down and they sat together on the felled tree-trunk.

"Who is the man?" he asked.

"I don't know. He is a friend of my father." Esther had controlled herself and her voice was calmer.

"But I thought your mother had agreed to send you to school for a little," Joseph said. "My father was speaking to her some days past."

"She would do so. It is my father who will not," Esther said, tears coming again, however hard she strove to hold them back. "He says there is no need for a woman to learn to read and write."

"But why a man from the lowland?" Joseph asked, seeking a way out. "There are many men here, where you need not go so far away from all who know you."

"He has asked for me and he is wealthy," Esther said simply. The explanation was enough.

"Joseph! I need that wood!" a woman's voice called shrilly. "Are you to be all day?"

Joseph rose and shouldered a bundle he had chopped.

"I will offer for you," he said bluntly. "Perhaps it is not too late. I will speak to my parents."

Esther looked up at him timidly. They had been children together all their lives, and the sudden transition from children to men and women had come very suddenly. But it had come, and her answer was curiously adult.

"They will never let you interrupt your schooling to care for me," she said, "and my father would not let me marry a son of your father. He is afraid of what people will say if we have much to do with a Christian preacher."

"But—what will you do?" Joseph said.

"What can I do?" Esther answered hopelessly. "Except go with this man."

Another, more insistent, shout came from the hill below and Joseph went. Esther, slowly and unhappily, went back across the stream to the mud house in its small compound. Her bare feet rustled in the dry grass and she wiped her tears away with the corner of her shawl. The hut was deserted. Her mother had gone to market and Tara must have gone with her. Esther sat, a small drooping figure, on the mud bench that ran around the walls of the hut outside and with a small stick scraped shapes that she pretended were letters such as she had seen in Joseph's school books, on the dusty ground.

Joseph's father was a weaver, although he ran a little school
for some of the local children once or twice a week. He was
known, half-mockingly, as 'the Evangelist' for he had been
for two years at a foreign mission school in the north, and
when he returned to his province he had brought a Bible,
and was very fond of talking about what it said to anyone
who would listen. Not that the teaching of the Bible was in
itself remarkable. The Christian Church had been established in the country many centuries ago, but the priests,
who sometimes taught the people, were fonder of telling
strange and wonderful fables than the plain truth of God s
word. Indeed, Esther had heard Joseph's father say that he
would be surprised if many of the priests in their little town
had even read the Bible itself. Esther had never been to his
school, but the Evangelist had a habit of gathering his
family and any of the neighbours who wished to come, for
evening prayers, after the day's work was done. Often at
that time, Esther would slip quietly in and listen, crouched
against the house wall, in the darkest place.

Two days after Esther had first heard of the proposed
marriage, Joseph's father saw her come in, and as he
opened the Bible he, knowing of her trouble, prayed inwardly for some message that would help her.

He chose to speak of the last gathering of Christ with the
disciples. He told how frightened and uncertain the disciples were about the future, and how Christ had reassured
them by saying that, although His body would leave them,
yet He was going to give them His Spirit, so that, in one
way, He would always be with them and not leave them
without comfort. When he had finished, he prayed for all
those who were afraid for the future, that they might know
the presence of Jesus Christ with them.

As Esther went out with the others, he followed her.
"May God give you health, child," he said kindly, laying a
hand on her shoulder to stay her a moment.

"And to you also, my father," Esther answered timidly.

"Come and sit down for a moment and talk," suggested the older man. "Are they expecting you at home?"

"My father's sister is ill and they went to her," she answered. "They will not be back before dark." They sat side by side on a rock. It was yet early evening: from this compound they could look down over the lowlands and across to the distant mountain peaks, dull red in the setting sun. Joseph's father left it to Esther to speak when she would and for some minutes there was silence.

"I am to be married, my father," Esther said at last. "I have heard it," he answered. "When is it to be?"

"On the feast day of St George. In ten days' time." A tear rolled slowly down her cheek and, despite her valiant efforts to control herself, a small sob escaped her.

The Evangelist did not look at her.

"Why don't you want to marry?" he asked her after a moment. "The man may be a good husband and you will be very happy. Is it not our custom to marry and have children?"

"I have seen the man who is to be my husband," Esther answered. "He was drunk and laughed much. He cannot read and does not want to, and he is as old as my father." It was an unchildlike summing-up of the situation and the man's brow creased.

"Have you told your parents that you do not wish to marry this man?"

"Many times," she said in a small voice, and added nothing, until after a pause she said, "What shall I do? Will you speak to my father?"

The Evangelist wondered whether to tell her that he had already spoken to both her parents and had asked that she be kept for his own son when he had finished at school, but without success and, indeed, with much rudeness, for what Esther had said to Joseph had been quite true. To be friendly with the Evangelist was no way to retain the approval of the local officials. With those steady dark eyes fixed upon him, he did not try to evade her.

"I have done so," he said simply, "but they wish for this marriage and will not hear of delay."

"It means a lot to them," admitted Esther. "I have found out the—my future husband is nephew to the Governor of one of the Southern provinces. But—I want to learn to read and write, and how can I, if I leave this place?"

The Evangelist sighed. "Why do you want to read, child? What women of your people read?"

"You ask me that!" Esther said. She rose and held out her hands for the big Bible that the man was still carrying. He gave it to her, surprised. She stood before him, holding it.

"You have told stories from this book," she said. "Stories of the Saviour of the world and how He was a man and loved people. I want to read them too."

"There is a verse," the Evangelist said, almost to himself, "that says 'thou hast hidden these things from the wise and understanding and revealed them to babes'." He got up and went into the house. Returning, he gently took the Bible from Esther and gave her in its place a small book. "Take this," he said. "It is part of this big book, and tells the story of the Saviour of the world, and when you have learned to read, you will be able to read it for yourself."

"But how can I learn to read?" Esther said miserably. "What scholar is there in the lowlands?"

"Ask God if He will find a way for you to learn," Joseph's father said solemnly. "Things which are impossible with men are possible with God."

"But where is God?" Esther cried, tears starting again. "I cannot speak to Him. I cannot see Him!"

There were voices near of approaching children. The Evangelist sat down again and pulled Esther to stand in front of him, holding her hands, clutching the precious book, in his.

"Learn this," he said very gently. "Say it after me. Jesus said,"

"Jesus said,"

"I will be with you always,"

"I will be with you always,"

"Even unto the end of the world."

"Even unto the end of the world."

"Is the lowlands at the end of the world?"

Esther shook her head.

"Then will our Lord Jesus Christ be with you there?"

"Yes."

"Then you may surely speak with Him. Say the words again."

"Jesus said, I will be with you always, even unto the end of the world."

2 · *Leaving Home*

OH HAPPY DAYS AT COLLEGE: *Will we ever see again*
Such zest of life, such fellowship, such striving after fame,
When every object brings a thought, and every thought a name.

Will we ever clatter noisily down staircases of stone,
Or linger in the library, half afraid to be alone,
Or curb a hot impatience at a tutor's dais drone?

But these short years will never come again to cheer our way,
For they are but the gateway and the dawning of the day.
And in the day's hard brightness, we will pause a while and say:

I remember when I dreamt of my achieving something great,
How my young shoulders stooped to bear imaginary weight,
And how I sought to comprehend the diverse work of fate.

But as I grew, experience enclosed my supple mind,
And crushed my keen aspirings, and sought my dreams to bind.
And said they were quite common to the youth of all mankind.

But when I sit and contemplate the years' increasing toll,
And my eyes have lost the vision of that near and glorious goal.
Will then I have, what now I lack: a peacefulness of soul?

I MET ANOTHER 'FRESHER' ON THE TRAIN. She was obviously
suffering from the inferiority complex which usually pre-
vails in young people being seen off by parents, especially
as I had involuntarily witnessed the affecting farewell.
However, once away, the hostility lessened and we talked
spasmodically, a mutual nervousness drawing us close
together. But presently a feeling of exultation and excitement overcame my misgivings at going to a new place, at
leaving home for the first time. University! The goal of my

youth and the gateway to my ambitions: the end of one
thing, but the beginning of so many others! Bath was
reached and finally, Bristol. It was pouring with rain. I
unloaded two large cases, a wireless, a hockey-stick, a
carrier-bag, and a handbag on to Temple Meads platform,
and began my University life.

Arriving at my Hall of Residence, I met my two neighbours, also freshers. We had a few days up at University
before the others came and we needed them, for it was all
rather overwhelming. That first night, dinner proceeded
with the quiet decorum of all first meals in the same circumstances. We were only a tiny group in the dining-hall, but
at least we had the advantage of knowing that we were all
new to it.

The following morning we all trooped down to the Victoria
Rooms. They were only ten minutes' walk away and we
assembled in the great hall. For the first time, the eight
hundred freshers were together. A grey-haired man, the
Vice-Chancellor, was introduced, and he got up to speak.
I was too excited to keep my attention from wandering,
but I heard a little: "You are the men and women who will
take positions of responsibility in future years. . . ." Oh,
there was that boy who was at the interview with me: so
he made it. ". . . to you and to those like you will be the
job of governing the country when . . ." That girl looks
familiar. She's wearing a Crusader badge. Now where
could I . . . "As students you have a debt to pay. Many of
you are here on public money: make full use . . ." That man
with a beard looks old: surely he can't be a fresher. ". . .
from school to University is a big step to take: take it
slowly. If you should find here that your work is not up to
standard, you may be asked to leave." (This produced some
rather nervous titters.) "This does not mean you are a
failure. It simply means you have chosen wrongly, and we
will do all we can to help you and ensure it does not happen
again." I wonder if there is a future Prime Minister here?

Or a Shakespeare? Or an Alexander Fleming? The Vice-Chancellor was now touching on religion. "This is not a secular institution. It is hoped that in your time here, every student will search for, and find, a Faith that will carry him through later life. The University makes no great demands upon its members. It requires you to go to church six times a year, at the beginning and at the end of each term, and it is to be hoped that this will not lay too heavy a burden upon those who have not yet acquired the habit of church-going." Was I really here? Was someone going to stand up in a minute and say, 'Helen Morgan, what are you doing here? Please leave!' It was over and we were going out for coffee. This feeling of unbelief that I had really arrived persisted right through my first year. It gave me a secret thrill every time I saw my name fairly and squarely on a notice board, even if it was merely for the purpose of reprimand, because I had failed to hand in an assignment on time.

Then, of course, there was the lovely feel of a gown, the crested note-paper and exercise books, the awed first visit to the Library, the first morning coffee at the Refectory (quite different from having it in a 'canteen') and the day when all the societies (there were ninety-six at that time) put up stalls and we went around them and decided what kind of a social life we wanted. Societies gave 'free teas' for anyone interested in finding out more about their activities. It became a matter of honour to see how many of these you could fit into an afternoon. We talked, we lounged on the Refectory steps and cast pitying glances at 'the public'. We tried to make our college scarves look less new, we clustered and looked with awe upon the various Professors and tutors as they were pointed out to us by the patronising seniors. We acted, in fact, like every year of freshers does, irrevocably convinced that we were the salt of the earth. And, in that first week, I joined the Christian Union, for I had been a Christian for four years when I went up to University.

When the others came up, we started being interviewed by those who were arranging our studies. I was reading for an English Honours degree, but all had to take a subsidiary subject for one year. I asked to take Latin.

The Professor of English, hearing this, surveyed my record in silence for a moment or two, and then said dryly:

"You know, Miss Morgan, it is a trifle unusual to—er—fail Latin quite as consistently as you have done during your schooling, and still petition to take it at University."

"I like reading it," I muttered, flushing.

"You wouldn't prefer Philosophy?"

I shook my head stubbornly.

"Good," he said suddenly. "Latin is a good partner to English Literature."

I was passed on to the Professor of Classics.

This is not a history of my three years at University. They were, on the whole, years in which I attained no great eminence. I strongly suspect the only time the Professor of my department noticed me, apart from the occasion mentioned above, was when I very nearly failed a paper in Anglo-Saxon in my first-part finals, and he wrote me a letter of rebuke and exhortation, hinting that unless my next year's paper on Middle English was unusually good, I would not get the degree 'of which I was capable'. I took the hint, and when I took that paper the following year, I was a competent, if temporary, authority on Chaucer, and practically knew 'Sir Gawaine and the Green Knight' by heart. For the one year's Latin, I was put in the bottom tutorial, under the instruction of a kindly elderly man who, after surveying one of my exercises, said, "It's a plain matter of choice, Miss Morgan. Either you learn the irregular verbs, or you change to Philosophy." I learnt the irregular verbs.

I wavered between various sports, and eventually decided to row. I never regretted it, and we had great fun at the boat club, despite the thinly-veiled contempt of the men's

club. We took a malicious pleasure in hearing the autocratic
cox shout, as the first eight stormed by our labouring four:
"Keep your eyes in thi-i-i-i-s boat! CONcentrate!!"
But they would relent sometimes and even condescend to
share a coach when we travelled to some regattas. I sang in a
500-strong choral society, where the Professor prowled
around at the most difficult parts of whatever we were
singing to see if we were on the right page. I painted
scenery for the Dramatic Society, and got covered in gold
paint. I paraded in a sheet and a laurel wreath as part of
one of the drays in 'Rag Week', and I continued as a
steady member of the Christian Union.

My real friends and daily companions were not members
of the Christian Union, though most of them belonged
to some other religious society; and what I considered to be
the narrow-mindedness of many of the C.U. members at
first surprised and displeased me. I had never met a Christian who thought it wrong to go to the theatre. I heard a
scornful, "Who? Mary Smith? Oh, she's one of those C.U.
types," on many lips in Hall and was not anxious to be so
labelled.

I joined the Anglican Society and often took communion
with them in the Cathedral: why should it worry me if they
ate wafers and not bread? Nevertheless, I was far too
grateful for the teaching offered by the C.U. to leave it, or
even cease to be an active member of it. I rarely missed a
Saturday night meeting. I remember to this day some of the
addresses that were given: addresses that kept us looking
forward to the future God had planned for us. What was
the future I had in mind those days? I don't think I knew
very clearly. I was too occupied in enjoying the moment:
the rambles in the country-side with friends, over the Mendip
Hills and into villages where, waiting hopefully at a bus
stop, we were told that there wasn't a bus until the following Tuesday; the coffee parties that went on late into the
night where conversation ranged over Eliot, Voltaire, the

modern theatre, and the problems of apartheid, predestina-
tion, and legal euthanasia; a trip abroad to the classic monu-
ments of old Rome and Florence; the adoration of Michel-
angelo; the sudden glimpses of hitherto unknown poets. I
wrote poetry of the naïve, untried kind of all University
poets. I was very happy.

After my first year at University, during the long vacation,
I was taken by a Christian friend to visit a friend of hers at a
missionary training college. We had been invited for tea,
and sat uncomfortably on a settee, balancing our plates on
our knees, and trying not to look at the enormous ugly oil-
painting that almost covered one wall. The impression I
received, and later recorded, though I ought to add I had
gone there in order to be critical, was that of plain, badly-
made-up women, whose conversation tended to be more
suited to the fifth form of a girls' school:

"Did you get your essay back?"

"Yes, but I only got 53 for it. Miss X was *livid*. She looked
furiously at me when I was going out today: suppose she
thought I should be swotting."

"Jane, Miss X says will you do an hour's gardening today
since you missed it on Tuesday."

"G-Gardening?" I said hesitantly. It was a damp cheerless
day.

"We all have to garden for an hour on Tuesday afternoons,"
Mary explained cheerfully.

I meditated. My companion was thinking of going there for
Bible training. "I don't know what the Lord intends for
me," was my inward thought, "but I'm never coming *here*
for Bible training!"

And then, one night, in my second year at University, I sat
on the floor of a crowded lounge, at a meeting of the Christian Union, when a Mr Len Adams of the Afghan Border
Crusade was speaking. Now I had come up to University
well warned about not being swept into missionary work.
"Never be 'called' in the emotional atmosphere of a mis-

sionary meeting," I was urged. "Keep your head. The Lord won't want you abroad." I quite agreed that this was likely. I wasn't the 'type'. Yet there in the darkness, we were looking at slides. I remember very little of what was said. I remember the missionary spoke of having a child born which died of small-pox while they were travelling to have it vaccinated. They had lived in a tent. He had nursed the child in one half, and, separated only by a canvas screen, his wife and their other children had lived in the other. Suddenly the Lord seemed to indicate, not in words, more in impulsion: 'That's the kind of work I want you to do.' I don't remember how it came, but I remember the response, the horrified response, I gave. I clenched my fists (it was dark) and cried out, almost aloud: "No, Lord. No!"

The moment passed and I pushed it aside, I thought, for ever. But the occasion is so clearly in my remembrance, even to the person sitting beside me at the time, that I cannot but feel that perhaps that was the real 'call' I received.

I decided to give missionary meetings a miss for the time being, but it was not long before another incident took place that forced me to think again. I had gone to a meeting, of which the theme of the talk was to be 'Christian Service'. The speaker told a story which I have never forgotten. The details are not in mind, but the theme was that of an old Christian warrior, who had been complimented by a young man on his great ministry, and he had replied sadly: "Yes, it is a great privilege to be used by God, but thirty years ago, I was called to the mission field and would not go, and all my life I have lived knowing that I have chosen God's second best." The words rang in my head . . . such a confession! Could it be that there were men of God, men in the Church, men who were apparently successful Christians living outwardly normal lives, but who were really living the life of the second best? Did I want God's second best? Did I? I walked home with some others. I stared at the silent houses. Under those roofs, were there men and women whom God had called abroad and who had refused His calling and chosen another? I remembered the picture of under-staffed mission stations that the speaker had painted, and thought of some of the lively Evangelical churches in Bristol. The proportion of workers was all wrong. Was *this* the reason?

"But I can't go unless I'm called," I remember saying in despair to an older girl, walking with me.

"You'll go, Helen," she said.

I was angry, indignant. How could she know? "But I can't unless I've been called," I said, holding firmly on to the offered straw. "But have I been called?" said a little insistent voice in my mind.

The following Easter I went to a Christian house-party, a student conference. I remember very little, except that I heard David Bentley-Taylor speak. For the very first time, it occurred to me that someone could actually *enjoy* being a missionary. He radiated enjoyment, he brought alive the people of whom he spoke, he evidently lived the scenes when he described them. I gradually crept further along the path of willingness and began to pray, "Lord, I will go if you want me to, but, Lord, you'll just have to make your calling clear, because I don't want to go—one bit."

And now I come to write down what I have told in detail to very few people, and even now, I write of it carefully, for I shrink from implying that everyone should experience such a call as mine, and I know that this definite call was granted me because of my weakness and not because of my strength.

It was a spring evening, late in April. I had recently begun to assist in a girls' club at my local church, near the Hall of Residence I lived in, and before I left, I knelt down to commit the evening briefly to God. It happened that my room commanded a wide view of the country-side and the window was wide open before me. I knelt by a book-case

and, inattentive as always, my eye fell on a book which I
had read often enough, by a missionary friend, about work
in India. I leafed through the pages idly and it brought, as
it often had, a vivid picture to mind, of work in India, of the
crying needs of that land. Suddenly a verse of poetry,
heading a chapter, caught my attention:

"Jesus, grant to us the vision
Of Thyself in intercession,
Pleading yet in Thy compassion
For each human soul."

I looked up and over the view before me. Suddenly, over
the country-side, over the trees and roof-tops of the city, a
new scene appeared: millions of men and women, indistinct,
but with hands that stretched to me and voices that seemed
to call for help. For one short second, a willingness, nay
more, a desire, to go welled up in me, overcoming all my
prejudices and hesitancies, overcoming all other thoughts.
I cried, perhaps aloud, "O Lord, call me!" Immediately I
spoke, I would have done anything to take the words back,
but it was too late for the answer had come, simply, un-
erringly, to my heart: "I am calling you!" Even at that
moment, my well-trained Christian Union-educated mind
was working: "Distrust 'voices from heaven'. Always back
up such 'visions' with the Word of God." My Bible was
handy and I caught it up. I verily believe that had I had no
confirmation from that, I could have ignored the occasion,
but the confirmation was there. In the hastily-opened Bible
flamed up the words in St Luke's gospel: "The harvest
truly is plenteous but the labourers are few." I gasped,
appalled at what had happened. In my one moment of
willingness (although I had not before thought I was unwilling) God had spoken. I arose from my knees with the
conviction upon me which has never yet left me. I was called
to the foreign mission field.

I remember a dear Church sister, who ran the club to which

I was going that night. I remarked to her, casually, that I
was going to be a missionary. She did not know that she
had the privilege of being the first person to know this!
For I did tell most people in time, even a somewhat
startled literary tutor. It was no good people saying, or
thinking, that I was 'not the type'. I agreed with that only
too heartily. I didn't think I was either, but if God did, then
I must not disobey. Basically, I think the firm resolve was
selfish. I wanted His best, and if this was it, as it appeared to
be, then nothing would prevent it. Then it was my third and
final year. To the most careless among us it was becoming
obvious that we now had to do something definite about
making our own way in this wicked world. The Education
year was an easy way of delaying the necessity for another
year. I applied.

"I'm sorry, Miss Morgan, but we do not find you a suitable
candidate for the Education department," said the department Head. She didn't add, though she might well have
done for I could see it in her eye, "You are not of the stuff
of which teachers are made."

I was quite astounded. Granted, I had wanted to enter the
department largely because of the thought of another year
of University life, and because of the large number of my
friends entering it, but I hadn't thought my motives had
been so obvious to the lecturers concerned with the appli-
cants. Out of the thirty of my class year who had applied, I
was one of the three who had been turned down. The others
were a boy who suffered badly from asthma and a girl who
almost certainly would fail her degree. It took some
swallowing.

I went to be interviewed by the University Appointments
Board.

"Well, Miss Morgan, if you would like to give me an
idea of the kind of job you're looking for . . . ?" said the clerk.

"I want a job for about two years," I said, "where I can do
the least amount of work for the most amount of money.

And I quite like the open air." I thought it was a good summing-up although it was obvious the clerk had heard it all before.

With finals on the way, however, I had other things to do than to worry about what the future held. Through May and June we laboured. The library, once a genial centre of quiet rustlings and invitations to coffee, became a tense place of electrified silences and frantic, furious glances cast at so much as a squeaking pen or a creaking chair. Enemies were made. There was a long queue at the requests for books-in-stock counter. There were locked doors from which the occupants only emerged for a brief five minutes to grab a plate of salad before diving back again. The awed, respectful glances of the first-years in some measure compensated for our sweat and toil, but even they showed resentment at being sworn at so often. We went down on our knees, metaphorically speaking, to borrow the notes of the more conscientious among us who had been consistently to lectures. In the Christian Union, we had talks on witnessing in times of stress, and of the importance of a quiet trust that God would justify the hours of study we had conscientiously given. And if I was getting side-glances from the more intimate of my friends, I tried to ignore them. I was a 'last-minute crammer' and always had been.

The term swept on and the examination entry-ticket arrived: to admit Miss Helen Morgan into the Great Hall. The last facts were committed to memory, the last prayer sent up, and it was on.

The exams themselves were sobering and it was hard to find a matter to joke on. The Great Hall, with its stone floor, was rather chilly, the rows of black-gowned students . . . I wonder if that chap knows he's got his gown on inside-out? . . . impressive and worrying. Out of several hundred, it was doubtful whether you could see many of your particular friends, and you were nearly bound to be beside one of the better scholars of your year, who settled

down with a determined air and began to fill pages with
neat, clear handwriting. There were lighter moments: for
example, when a young, eager tutor strode impressively
down the Hall between the rows of desks, forgetting his long,
wide-sleeved gown which neatly cleared three or four desks
and swept the papers from under the pens of the students
into one glorious muddle on the floor. The red-faced tutor,
joined by the iron-faced invigilator, sorted it all out while
the students concerned waited with patient, forbearing
faces. We found it mildly entertaining: but on the whole it
was a case of slogging on until it was finally finished and we
could spend the last week sadly clearing up, preparatory to
finding out what the world had to offer us.

★

ESTHER'S WEDDING DAY CAME. She had not run away for she
did not know where to run to, but she turned over plan
after plan in her mind. The only person she knew who might
receive her was her father's sister, and she was ill, and in
any case, they would search for her there. She had had one
scene with her father, when she had begged him to change
his mind but he had remained firm and on her bursting
into tears and attempting defiance, he had simply beaten
her, hard and efficiently, for he had often thrashed his
sons. She had not spoken on the subject since.

"Esther! Get up!" her mother called. "This is no day to
stay lying down. You must go and borrow the glasses from
our neighbours."

She dressed slowly and ate some of the parched corn her
mother held out to her. Her father was nowhere to be seen
but she knew he would be slaughtering the sheep for the
wedding feast. Her mother looked at her with a certain
compassion.

"Did you not sleep?" she asked. "You must not be afraid.
Your future husband is a man of much wealth and you
will have a great position. And when you have children,

you shall bring them back here that we may see them."
Esther did not answer but went slowly out to borrow glasses
from the huts around, for these were communal property in
times of feasts. She experienced much good-humoured
jesting and greetings from the neighbours and her own
downcast countenance was nothing remarkable. Every
bride was expected to be sad and solemn on her wedding
day. They worked all morning: even little Tara was grinding the spices to be used in the main dishes. Soon the hut
was swept, skins spread over the mud benches around the
sides, and wooden benches borrowed and set out; branches
were strewn on the floor, and a kind of curtain erected
behind which the bride must sit. The bridal dress, tradition-
ally the gift of the bridegroom, arrived with a number of his
friends and Esther was dressed carefully, her hair braided
and freshly anointed with oil. Then she was led behind the
curtain as the guests began to arrive.

The day seemed interminable to her. She remained unseen
by most of the guests. Food was brought to her by Tara
and another cousin, who were waiting on her and sharing
her isolation. She was, of course, only just cut off from the
guests and could see them through the thin curtain, better
than they could see her. There was eating and drinking,
jovial story-telling, and even some dancing by the younger
guests. As the sun began to sink towards the hills, a new
sound was borne to her: laughter and singing, the sound of
mules' bridles and the beating of drums. As it grew nearer,
she knew only too well what it was. The bridegroom
and his party were arriving, climbing the hill that led
from the town to their little cluster of huts. Esther shud-
dered and dropping her head into her hands she began
to sob. Those who were near enough to the curtain to
hear her against the noise of the celebrating men, smiled
indulgently. All brides behaved like this. It was to be expected. Tara, much troubled, moved closer to her sister and
patted her arm, staring into her face. Esther put an arm

around her and wept afresh. God knew she had had little
enough childhood, few hours of playing as western children
might play, but such as it was, it was over now. The house
filled with noisy, laughing young men and her mother came
to prepare her for the journey.

The mule was white and the red bridle gleamed and jingled
in the afternoon sun. Because of the long journey back to the
bridegroom's home, they were to start almost immediately
in order to have made some part of the descent before
nightfall. They were to spend the night with some relations
of the groom, who lived on a kind of immense 'shelf' in the
great cliffs. It was a small village and a useful one to those
who could not ascend or descend in one journey. It was, in
fact, in sight of Esther's home, although so far away that the
clusters of huts looked like stones and the only real indication of the village was that the sun would catch the tin
roof of the church at certain times of day. So Esther came to
look for a second time upon her bridegroom's face.

He was short, but strongly built, appearing almost fat
amongst the sinewy leanness of his countrymen and companions. He was much older than Esther.

"I will never be his wife," she thought, looking at the lines
on his face while he apparently kept everyone in a gale of
merriment. He was dressed in a European-style coat,
evidently considering this the height of fashion, and on his
head was a yellow, plastic, brimmed-hat. Sweat, in this hot
afternoon, rolled down his forehead and his voice boomed
confidently:

"So this is my little bride whom I have come so far to
fetch," he said and his eyes devoured her. Her flesh shrank
and she stared at him as a creature of the wilds might stare
at the hunter who advances upon a trap.

Fortunately, his friends closed about him, the elders advanced who would see to the closing of the bargain, and
Esther could cling frantically to her mother without the
witnesses seeing her.

"Mother, don't let me go," she whispered despairingly. "I cannot leave home with him: he doesn't want me. What use can I be to him? Oh, mother, save me!"

Esther's mother was a woman and the plea did not leave her unmoved, but she too had left her home when she was but a child and knew no other future for her daughter than this. But she took Esther's arm from about her waist gently, and whispered:

"I have a sister in Engadi. If you are too ill-treated, or if he turns you away, do not come back here for your father would not receive you again, but try to go to my sister and she will help you."

"I will remember," Esther said more steadily for this did more than anything to make her realise that there was no way out except what she could devise.

Her father came out. "It is done," he said, and then, looking sternly at Esther, he added harshly, "Make him a good wife, child. There is no home for you here if you do not."

She did not answer, nor did she look at him.

They lifted her to the white mule amid shouts and song. Her box was strapped to another. Neighbours called greetings and came to kiss her farewell. Finally, Tara, tears streaming down her face, was put beside her to ride a little way with her. Over the head of this little sister, Esther raised her head to look at the home she was leaving. It was not much: a cluster of mud huts with their straw roofs, surrounded by a brush-wood fence, but it was all she knew of home and held the only people she loved. She kissed her mother and they lifted Tara down.

"Now let us ride," said one of the young men around her. "The sun is low in the sky." They hastened the mules on-wards. Esther's tears dried. Her child's face set stubbornly. This was the time for which she had planned during the past weeks. Her mother's words had fanned the resolve into flame and she was waiting, tense, for the moment she could put her plan into action.

Their way lay at first over a long unbroken plain, for they had to reach the only way of descent, and it was early evening before they came to the other side of the plain and could turn at last into the west, where the lowlands lay. While they were near villages they kept up the festivities of a bridal party and chanted and waved greetings to those who bowed their good wishes. The man who would be her husband had left Esther alone, only looking at her consideringly now and again. His brother rode beside her, holding the rein of her mule lightly in his hand, and some four or five others trotted beside. Finally, the last of Esther's friends fell away and she heard their voices echoing in the distance. At the same moment she felt her mule's head go down. They were descending. Her heart beat painfully, but she waited. This part of the land was familiar to her and had been from her youth for as a young child she had played in this gorge, and sometimes had accompanied her brothers in the tending of cattle. At a place where the path was level for a moment, she murmured her request to the man at her side. He nodded. For a moment they all halted and one of the men helped her down from the mule. She glanced shyly at them and disappeared behind a boulder. There were some grins at this and the groom made as if to follow her in game, but they waited. And Esther, tying her long skirt tightly so that it could not trip her, began to run.

She had a good start before they realised she had gone, but then, thanks to the new bridal dress, they saw her bounding lithely across the hillside and shouts reached her ears. But she did not falter. Across the hillside she ran, until the river bed was reached and then down the river bed, leaping on well-remembered boulders, unerring in her choice. Fear lending her wings, she flew on, still down, and away from the path where she had left the bridal party. Where the river fell into a deep gorge in its downward flow, she left it on the left and began again to run along the side of the mountain. She knew of a narrow and dangerous path which led to the lowlands and intended to reach it. Once having gained that part of the cliff face, she knew she would be safe from pursuit. It would be impossible to search closely the many caves, gullies and hiding places of that area.

The sun was low now, and great black shadows were cast by the rocks she passed. Suddenly a shout made her pause, for it was directly above her. Breathing heavily, she stopped and stared upwards. There, high up, were a number of men beginning to descend towards her. She realised that the bridal party were in visual contact with them and the shouts she had heard were enlisting their aid. There was only one way left to her and she took it.

Back the way she had come, running, half-walking now, she once again disappeared from sight into the steep-sided gorge. Through the thorny bushes of the mountain side she pushed her way, across the river and along the other side, towards the precipice known as the cliffs of the monkeys. Suddenly she heard a new sound, nearer her than any yet, and, turning, she saw a man following her and she recognised, with a fresh flood of terror, that it was her groom. He had shed his coat and his white shirt was torn from a shoulder, but he was grinning at her, almost, she thought dizzily, revelling in the chase. He seemed to have left his friends behind, or perhaps they had separated not knowing her path. There began the most painful and desperate race yet. Esther was young and knew the ground but she had run twice the distance of her pursuer and she felt she must surely fall soon. The man following, although he did not know the paths, had been bred on such country and he did not falter in the pursuit but steadily gained on her. She must recross the river, Esther thought, but she must be dangerously near the edge of the great falls where the river finally reached the main descent of the cliffs and fell in a great cascading roar to the pools far, far beneath. If she did not recross she would surely be trapped on the cliff edge itself. Making up her mind, she plunged downwards over the shoulder of the hill, sliding and slipping. She emerged again where the river was flowing unhurriedly between rocks and pools towards the fall. She was very near the edge of the cliff, and, instinctively, knowing the danger of the cliff pool, she turned upstream before leaping across the rocks. Then, just as she had gained the other shore, the bushes parted and the man appeared. They both paused, staring at each other, she in terror, he in anger, but they did not speak. The noise of the water made it impossible, even had their heaving breasts permitted of speech. Finally, he plunged down, straight down to the treacherous cliff pool that looked so easy to cross but which hid in its dark depths such menace. For a fraction of a second, Esther realised what would happen and started forward in renewed horror, but the breathless shout was not on her lips before there was the sound of slipping and a shout that rose above the thunder of the falls. With eyes wide open with horror, and forgetting everything but the need of helping the stricken man, Esther went down on her hands and knees and crawled towards the pool.

The cliff pool was the last check the water had before its long descent. The walls of the pool were sheer for about ten feet and then gradually sloped outwards, so that the approach to the pool could only be safely made by crawling flat on your face. The rocks, covered when the river was in flood, were grey and smooth. The pool was generally believed to be bottomless and was surrounded on all sides by the rock walls. The only exit was the dreadful lip over which the water spilled to the lowlands, two thousand feet below. Esther lay flat and inched forward until she could look down. Her bridegroom had some elementary knowledge of swimming and was still afloat, scrabbling desperately at the smooth walls with his hands, splashing dementedly away from the lip over which the water flowed so deceptively gently.

"Help me!" he cried, when he saw Esther's head appear

outlined against the pale evening sky. "For God's sake, help me!"

Esther stared around. Not a movement on the quiet hills. All pursuit had left them long ago. All the cattle had been rounded up and taken home. They were near no pathway or road on which might be travellers. But she found her voice and raised it in the high call for help which was well-known in all parts of the country . . . except where it cannot be heard above the roar of a water-fall. Again and again she cried, meanwhile taking off her long shawl, even her dress. She knotted them together, and, holding one end herself, she threw the other down to the drowning man. He grasped it and immediately applied such strength that Esther was dragged to the very edge of the vertical fall before she let go, just in time to save herself from falling.

She heard a hoarse, despairing cry as she did so and her head swam with dizziness. She was lying in a dangerous position, her head much lower than her feet, spread-eagled on the rock. Inch by inch she moved backwards, shutting her ears to the faint noises coming from the pool. Once safe, she sprang to her feet and ran screaming up the mountain side, first one side and then the other until she was too exhausted to do anything but throw herself to the ground and lie there, her chest and her heart heaving and beating until she thought she would die. No one had heard her: no one had witnessed the dreadful scene. There was no sound above the sound of water now and she knew, without needing to approach the pool again, that her chosen husband, from whom she had fled, was dead. She lay face downward, in a little dried-up gully that led into the river, clad now only in a thin white underslip which she had been given for the wedding: only it was white no longer. All the emotion of the day, the long tensed-up morning, the ride, waiting for the moment of escape, the desperate chase and now the death of the man she had feared, burst out and great sobs racked her body and her fingers dug into the dusty ground, and over all, the noise of the water rose, and grew great, and filled her ears until she knew nothing more. The howl of a hyena brought Esther fully to her senses. She sat up listening. It sounded again. She found herself shivering violently. It was nearly dark. With all the self-control she could muster, she controlled her shallow breathing. She was alone and it was nearly night: she must decide what was the best thing to do. Certainly, she could not stay there: she glanced involuntarily and with a shudder in the direction of the pool and then got to her feet. She was still not far from her own home, but she could not go back. By this time the story of her flight would be known there; perhaps the relations of the man would have gone back to demand the return of the bride-price, and in any case, surely they would come seeking him here. They knew the way he had gone. Slowly, she began to walk away from the highlands. The path on which she had left the men was barred to her, but she knew of another some distance off leading from a distant town, along which traders often passed, descending to the lowlands. She would find a cave or shelter under a rock near the path and beg whoever passed first to take her down with them wherever they were going. Finally recrossing the river, she stopped and drank. For the first time she felt hungry and she was shivering uncontrollably in the thin cotton dress. There was just light enough for her to see her path as she climbed the shoulder of the hillside. Surely it was too light yet for leopards and hyenas to advance on men . . . or was it? Her heart bounded, as right from under her feet, a great baboon sprang up and leapt away chattering angrily. Finally, her tired feet found a narrow path. If she followed it, it would bring her to the wider mule road. She hurried on, tense for movement of wild life around her. When at last she reached the wider road, it was quite dark, and the only light was the thin crescent moon.

She had never been out at night before: night was the domain of the bandits and the wild animals, and she crouched in the poor shelter of an over-hanging rock. Hugging herself with her bare arms, she suddenly felt against her waist, where she had bound it in the morning, the little book that Joseph's father had given her, and she fingered it. His gentle voice came back to her, and she whispered: "Jesus said, I am with you always, even to the end of the world." and remembered the Evangelist's words, "Then you may surely speak to him." So she looked at the moon which seemed the most friendly thing she could see just then, and said unsteadily, for she was still shivering, "Send some travellers, Lord, to take me away from here."

She heard them when they must have been miles away, for voices carry far when thrown by mountains. They were voices of men raised in laughter and shouts. Presently, she could see pin-points of lights bobbing up towards her and hear the horses' hoofs on the rocks. It was a big party. She could not guess why they should, against all custom, be travelling at night. At first she thought they must be bandits, but dismissed this thought. Bandits did not travel with this amount of noise. They drew nearer until she could see against the torchlight the black forms of the travellers . . . traders, she saw at once, banded together with guards to protect them through the dangerous, unlawful country ahead. She stepped out on the track and waited, so that they would see her in good time. They saw her and the first man pointed a rifle at her.

"Don't shoot," Esther said tremulously. "I am alone here." The men drew around her, pulling their mules and horses to stop, looking her up and down and Esther, conscious of her bare arms and thin dress, hung her head and waited for them to speak.

"By St Michael, a new kind of hyena!" a thick voice said. "It stands on its hind legs." There was some laughter: the men had drunk well that night. One of the men, perhaps the leader, stiffly dismounted.

"A light!" he ordered roughly, and one was brought. The man advanced toward Esther and took her by the arm, pulling her into the full light of the flaming torch. Then he let her go.

"What do you here?" he said, and his voice was not friendly. "Did your man tire of you on the journey, or have you friends hidden in these hills waiting to fall on us?"

Esther had her story ready. "My husband beat me," she said faintly. "I ran away but the night overtook me and I am very afraid. Take me with you until we reach a place of shelter."

"Your husband's name and country?"

She was silent, not knowing the best thing to say.

Another man pushed forward. "She is only a child, Joshua," he said more kindly. "She can tell us her story in the morning. Let us take her. She will die on the hillside overnight."

"Yes, let us take her," another man rumbled sleepily from his mule. "We are not due home for three nights yet: a woman is not amiss."

"You are too trusting, brother," the leader said angrily. "What woman who is innocent would be out in such a dress at such a time?"

"No woman of the streets, that's certain," another put in. "They're all tucked up in bed by now, earning their breakfast."

There was another chuckle.

"My husband snatched at my shawl as I fled," Esther said timidly. "Oh, do not leave me here, my masters. I am so afraid." Tears and fear filled her voice and the man who had spoken kindly came up.

"Come, little one," he said. "Ride behind me until we reach shelter. I have a shawl bought for my wife. It is not made up yet but no matter."

He loosened the straps of his baggage for a moment to take out a thick shawl. Esther clutched it thankfully around her. "Come then," he bade her and stretched down his hand to her.

"Your wife will have something to say if you ride in with a woman from the market," grumbled the leader. "It is not part of our business to encourage a woman to leave her husband . . . but I agree we cannot leave her here. She shall come with us and we will decide what is to be done with her in the morning."

The party moved forward and Esther rode behind the man who had taken her part, with tears of thankfulness rolling down her face to be leaving the place that held so many memories of fear for her.

They stopped finally at a compound where they were evidently expected, even if it were the middle of the night, for the gates were pushed open and a sleepy and scolding old woman began bustling around them. Esther felt herself lifted from the saddle and laid down on a hut floor, but by this time she was too exhausted to care and sank at once into the deep sleep of the young and weary. Around her, the men too flung themselves down, drank coffee and then slept while the younger of them tended the animals.

When she awoke, it was daylight and the smell of a cooked meal was filling the air. Men were stretching and picking themselves up from the floor. In the darkness of the hut, her movement had not been seen, but presently she sat up and a man called out to her, "Well, child? How has the night passed?"

She answered timidly and conventionally. "May God be praised."

Hearing her voice, the man whose voice she recognised as the Joshua of the previous night came over to her.

"You are indeed a child," he said, staring at her. "What shall we do with you? What have you in mind for yourself? Have you a home? Where are you going?"

"I have no home. I am going to the lowlands," she said, answering the two last questions.

"But to whom?"

"I know nobody. I shall work."

He smiled unpleasantly. "Do you know the only work for such as you?"

Esther dropped her eyes. "I had thought of working in a household," she said.

"That . . . in certain households . . . should not be too difficult to arrange," he said and thought a moment. "You may come with us as far as Mulata," he said then: "it is the biggest town on our route and should be the best place for you. Unless, that is, you wish to serve one of the men of this caravan?"

Esther felt the blood rise up to her face.

"I will gladly wait on you all, sir," she said. "But I will not sell myself until I know there is nothing else to do."

She rode behind Joshua for the next two days and they reached Mulata towards the evening of the second day. When they reached the market place of the town, Joshua signed to her to get down.

"Our country is farther on and we must reach the next village before nightfall," he said, looking down at her. "Have you any money?"

She shook her head. He reached in his pocket and gave her fifty cents. She took it and bowed. He rode on. Esther waited until the man who had given her the shawl passed. Then she took it off and held it out. He reined in his mule. "Keep it, child," he said. He looked down at her with troubled eyes. She looked small and defenceless, her hair still braided as it had been for the wedding. "I could give you a home," he said. "My wife would be kind to you."

She tried to smile at him. "I am well enough," she said. "May you travel on in peace."

He frowned, but shook his bridle and moved on. She stood, a forlorn little figure, in the middle of the road, clutching two twenty-five cent pieces. Less than forty-eight hours ago she had been a bride, then a widow before the marriage was truly made. Now she stood, over two days' journey from her home, alone and friendless.

"I am with you always," she said to herself, "even to the end of the world."

★

AND SO WE LEFT HOME: I, going willingly to a sheltered seat of learning, to a place where there were men ready to guide and help me towards maturity: Esther, thrust out terrified to a life where she alone, under God, held the reins to direct her future. I, concerned to enjoy myself, resenting the interference of God's hand of direction even while I yielded to it: Esther, not knowing that life was there to be enjoyed, concerned only to live without starvation, without dishonour, fumbling uncertainly towards the little she knew of God.

I was seventeen when I first lived away from home: Esther was not yet twelve.

3 · Working

I FLUNG MYSELF into a chair in the smoke-filled staff room. Outside could be heard the joyful, uninhibited noise of departing pupils. It was 4 pm on a Friday afternoon.

"If somebody else doesn't get there first," I declared grimly, "I shall strangle young Edwards with my own hands."

The Senior Master smiled at me and poured me out a cup of tea.

"If thoughts were actions I should think half that form would be dead by now," he remarked. "What's he been doing?"

"What hasn't he?" I said gloomily. "He started before I got there by polishing the blackboard with black shoe-polish, and ended by throwing a milk bottle at Gray, which went through the window."

More staff arrived.

The English Head of Department (curtly): "Helen, don't forget you're doing detention tonight. Here's the book."

The Geography teacher who, with me, doubled as Games mistress (briskly): "You're umpiring the second XI match tomorrow, Helen. The coach will be here to collect us at 9 am."

A fifth-form boy (unctuously): "Please, Miss Morgan, you've given us prep on *Macbeth* and you've still got our exercise books."

The Senior Mistress (ominously): "Miss Morgan, was it in your class that the third-form window got broken?"

A first-form girl (innocently): "Please, miss, you forgot to give us any homework tonight."

The School Secretary (politely): "I don't seem to have received your dinner register today, Miss Morgan."

A third-form boy (indignantly): "Why've you put me in detention again, miss? I didn't do nothing!"

Thus me, immersed (and never was there a more accurate word) in my first job.

I had heard from the Appointments Board of the University, just two days after I had had my interview. They enclosed a letter from a headmaster in a small town in the midlands. He wanted a teacher, was prepared to take a graduate straight from University, suggested that two or three years would be quite sufficient, and said the job was mainly English teaching, but also games. Was I interested?

I went to see the place during my last week at University. Getting there was an eye-opener to country transport: a two-hour wait here, another somewhere else, the necessity to go right out of my way to reach my destination and finally a bleak, windswept landscape on every side. It was my first view of the English midlands. And my first impression was that Hereward the Wake was welcome to it. However, I somehow felt it was the right place, and, after a somewhat nervous summer holiday, I embarked on the teaching profession, inwardly bearing in mind the plump grey-haired mentor of the Education Department and her views on my teaching potentialities.

I was, I know now, immensely fortunate in my first school. It was then only about 300 strong, and the accommodation was poor, but the headmaster was first class, and the senior mistress was new at the same time as I was, a great advantage, for she took (naturally) a while to get settled in, by which time I had some feet of my own to stand on. I arrived for the start of the autumn term, the night before, and met the senior English master, Robin, at the school. He was rather brusque in manner, but friendly and ready to help me where he could. We looked vaguely at the stock cupboard with its piles of *The Mill on the Floss* and *A Tale of Two Cities*.

"Here's a syllabus," he said, "but take what books you like."

I opened a grammar book. The chapter heading was "The Preposition", but the next words after that were: "Select the propositions in the following sentences."

I swallowed.

"You know, I don't really know much about grammar," I said weakly. "It—er—it doesn't seem to come into a University English Course, does it?"

"You'll learn," he said laconically. "Just keep a page ahead of them."

We went back to the deserted staff room and collected our coats.

"Oh, there's just one thing," he said, and a shade of embarrassment crept into his tone. "The coming fifth form has a number of extremely difficult boys. The only thing to do is to divide the form, or the rest of them will never get their exam at the end of the year. I'm afraid you will have to take the lower half." He smiled apologetically. "It's one of the misfortunes of being new."

Next day, school started. I was given my timetable. Robin escorted me to my first class, a thirty-five-strong second form, and opened the door for me.

"Just remember two things," he said. "You must be master of every situation, and you know everything." And on those two pearls of truth, my teaching career started.

The first months of such a career are bound to be fraught with difficulties. Mistakes are made, punishments are misused, every Friday afternoon is a torment. Night after night, you sit down to a pile of exercise books before you realise that it is not essential to read *every* word of every composition. But there were things that made it easy for me: comfortable and happy digs, genial and sympathetic colleagues, and a headmaster who was kindly and steadfastly behind all I did.

It was the fifth form that gave me the most trouble. They were all boys, as Robin had warned me, and how they ever got into a grammar school was a constant puzzle to me.

Several of them towered over me in height, and when they changed from their school blazers into khaki (which they did every Friday afternoon when the Boys' Army Corps assembled) I felt that to press home the finer points of Hardy's *Under the Greenwood Tree* would be beyond the capabilities of anyone. I had not, until that year, been in favour of corporal punishment, but I became then a firm believer in it. After the headmaster had caned two of the biggest boys on my behalf (fortunately he himself was over six feet) things were much better. However, by the second year, these same boys had become cheeky but very nice errand boys about the town, and I was fast forgetting the fights I had had with them.

I found life in the country had many attractions. The church, though not evangelical in the sense I had learned to use the term, was yet a happy fellowship, and I found plenty to do within it. I found Christians there who were real Christians without ever having read John Stott's *Becoming a Christian*! They could testify, not, indeed, to any sudden conversion, but nevertheless, they had found a faith that meant something to them. One spoke, when pressed, of his work in the fields: how he had watched the ever-changing miracle of the sky and thus come to think of its Creator. He spoke awkwardly, never having heard the words 'my testimony'; but his whole life demonstrated that he knew God as more than simply the Creator. He was one of a number. They were simple, kindly, sincere, and I learnt much from them.

But my missionary call did not fade. Interested in the job, and contented as I was, this period of teaching was never more than an interval of two years before I would enter training for the mission field.

All the books said that the best time to apply to a missionary society was a year before one desired to enter training. Accordingly, towards the end of my first year, I began to consider which missionary society I should offer my services to. My eventual choice was a singularly unheroic affair. There was no voice from heaven, or great moment of decision. I had taken a mild interest in one society for a number of years, but I had links with two others and hesitated for a time between them. Then I went to a youth week-end organised by the first society, and during it, went for a walk with one of the 'elders' of the society. Learning of my state of indecision, he dismissed the two other societies in two brief sentences and recommended his own. Surprisingly, for I never took well to advice, I drifted without particular enthusiasm towards that society. I never received, in the years following, any indication that it was the wrong choice for me.

I might answer now some of the queries that people have as to the way you get into a missionary society. There are, first, the 'candidate's papers', a formidable number of them, dealing with everything from how many G.C.E. subjects you did or did not take, to what you believe about the Holy Communion service. It is worth taking a copy of what you wrote down then and reading it up before you go for your interviews, or you will probably contradict yourself. I remember being stuck at the first question in my papers which read: "What circumstances led you to desire to become a missionary?" I felt that I ought, in fairness, to point out that I had never desired to become a missionary, and that I didn't now desire to become a missionary. I was simply obeying the call I had heard from the Lord in the matter. Then there are a number of references and testimonials that have to be given by your friends and your employers. These I have never seen, of course, nor have I had to fill out any for anyone else, but I remember the look on my headmaster's face when he had been so engaged. We strolled across the playground while I wondered what misdemeanour I had committed. Then he said: "Well, I've done my best for you . . . but I did point out that some of the questions asked are things no headmaster *ought* to know

about a member of his staff!" He left me with a still un-
satisfied curiosity about those questions!

Interviews, which come next, took place in July. I had four,
I believe, and three of them took place on the same day,
with no interval for lunch: the interviewer before lunch
assuming that I would have it with the next, and the
interviewer after lunch, who lived quite a distance from the
first, assuming that I had already eaten. I suffered in silence.
I thought it was perhaps some kind of endurance test. I
remember now very little about those interviews. I recall
the look on a clergyman's face when I announced that there
were seven sacraments . . . the enormity of the crime was
only made clear to me much later on. From then on, when
in the presence of officials of the society, I endeavoured to
carry under my arm a copy of *The Catholic Faith*, an 'ap-
proved' book on evangelical Anglican doctrine. I remember
being asked to relate the details of my 'call', which I had
never done to anyone before. I complied with considerable
emotional stress, much alleviated by the fact that my listener
was forced to pay the milk bill, order bread, and answer the
phone while I was talking. I remember a lady saying, "I
think somehow that you will not find a missionary training
college very easy". No doubt she was looking at my ear-
rings. I remember that I got thoroughly fed up and sick of
talking about myself for the first time in my life. Then I
waited, while the society's wheels slowly turned.

I received the letter of acceptance at Christmas. I was
expecting it around that time, and had diligently searched
through *Daily Light* to find a day I considered suitable for
receiving the glad tidings on. But when the letter did come,
I read it through, and then turning automatically to my
next letter, I opened it. It was from a friend who had the
vaguest knowledge of the details of my present situation,
but from the envelope fell a small card. I picked it up.
There were two words written on it: "Yes, Lord." I had
prayed the Lord would give me an especial verse just then

and this was it. Not protestations of faith and love, not a
vision of future dangers and future triumphs. I cast out of
my mind the heroics of the business, and simply repeated
those two words: "Yes, Lord." And they rang in the air
around me until for that moment the whole sky seemed to be
rejoicing with me.

I was now an 'accepted candidate'. One step had been
taken in the right direction. Now to cut the ties of my school
and to enter the famous Missionary Training College,
ironically, the very one I had visited with such disastrous
impressions four years before. Ties are not easy things to
cut. This must be obvious from the number of 'called and
dedicated' future missionaries that leave University every
year and who, in five years' time, are settled in this country
without apparently any thought of leaving for foreign climes.
There is almost certainly going to be the question of
marriage, and I did not escape this for I never had any
cloistering impulses in that direction, and certainly did not,
in the two years of teaching in a mixed school, cut myself
off from the opposite sex. However, I usually remembered to
label myself pretty firmly 'for export only' which acted as a
kind of brake. There is the question of money. Three years'
penury as a student is a good preparation for having real
pay coming in. Going back to student finances has its
difficulties. And there is ambition. You, in concert with
your contemporaries, are entering a career. Two years have
seen you settled in, beginning to enter a position of trust,
possibly of further responsibility. Now you are to become
again a student, a junior, and a learner. Knowing now
stories such as that of Esther, which runs beside this narra-
tive of mine, I can find it in my heart to be ashamed at the
conscious sense of self-righteousness with which I 'gave up'
the things enumerated above, and entered the training college. The admiration of my friends that I should willingly
do this was very pleasing. I admired myself. Only afterwards, when you realise the struggle so many others have

just to live, do such 'sacrifices' seem trivial and shallow, not worthy of the tears and heart-burning that they caused us. I left school, and the little midland town of which I had become so fond, and returned to college life, no longer 'Miss Morgan', teacher of senior English at a grammar school, but 'Helen', first-year student, and missionary candidate at a missionary training college. I arrived one September evening. When the taxi left me at the gate of the college, I paused a moment and looked it over, mentally promising myself:

"They'll never succeed in making *me* into their pattern!"

*

ESTHER LIFTED THE HEAVY JAR in which the beer was kept and poured it carefully into the old kettle. It was early evening but already there were a number of men in the house talking loudly in competition with the strident dance music on the radio.

"Esther, bring in that roasted bread you made this afternoon," called Sidara from within the house.

"Get a move on with that drink, will you, girl?" grumbled a man lurching past her to relieve himself in the tiny backyard.

"Esther, just you tell Sidara to give me back my oil lamp right away," called a neighbour through the wooden slats of the fence. "We need it."

"I'll bring your lamp in one moment, Dessie," Esther answered to this last speaker and picking up the kettle, she went into the hot, smoky interior of the house.

She knelt to pour the beer into the tall glasses which stood on a tray on the mud floor and then offered them one by one to the men seated on the rough wooden benches or wicker chairs around the tiny room. Then she brought a tin plateful of roasted bread and placed it on a low table, and finally picked up a small unlit oil lamp which they had borrowed the night before. Thus Esther, in her first job.

When the traders had left she had begun to walk slowly up the street. It was the time of day when work was over and the women were sitting on the doorsteps of the rough mud houses, or on the stones that edged the track, talking with their neighbours. The noise of a radio was heard from one drink-house and a hubbub of noise and laughter. Esther saw the eyes of the women considering her and quickened her step. They would know she was a stranger but perhaps they would think she was visiting a relation. She did not want to ask for work where they had seen her arrive. She turned up a dry, dusty path between the trees and stopped by a group of women sitting idly at the gate of a row of houses.

"May God give you health," she said.

They responded, and the greetings went easily backwards and forwards. Then, as the women turned again to their own talk, Esther said breathlessly.

"I am looking for work."

"What kind?" one asked her.

"I can cook and carry water and serve the house-owner," Esther said.

"We can all do that, my child," said a fat jolly-looking woman. "What is your trouble? Haven't you a home?"

"I am an orphan," Esther said.

"And your man has cast you out?" another said, fingering the thick shawl. "This was not begged for I think."

"A traveller on the road from the highlands gave it to me," Esther answered. "I have no man."

"She came with the traders from the highlands," volunteered a small boy who had joined the group. "I saw her."

"Well, if you came with them, why did you not go with them?"

"I do not belong in their company," Esther said wearily.

There was a pause. Then one said, "Have you a husband who will seek you here and blame us if we give you shelter?"

"I have no husband," Esther answered, her voice trembling a little. "And I have no home."

A young woman pushed forward.

"Come home with me," she said with rough compassion. "You can make yourself useful and I daresay be worth your keep."

Esther looked at her. She was some years older than Esther but still young, and she wore a European style dress with a low neck. She had dangling ear-rings and her trade was obvious enough. But Esther was not in any position to choose and the woman's eyes were kind. Besides she was desperately hungry and her head was aching.

There were some chuckles as they went off together.

"She'll put you out of business, Sidara," one called.

"Don't listen to them, child," Esther's guide said in irritation.

She led the way down the wide mule track, walking swiftly with long graceful strides and Esther followed her humbly, not seeking to talk. Some men called out greetings to her, and she replied good-humouredly. Presently they were among dark alleys and then were back on the main street by which Esther had entered the town. Here were the usual rows of mud houses, thinly divided by mud and wood walls. In most of them were groups of men, whose voices could be heard talking amongst themselves cheerfully: these were the drink houses. In some sat young women who had as yet no customers. They seemed unworried, lounging against their door posts and watching the passers by. To them, Sidara spoke, and they answered with their eyes on Esther. At last Sidara stopped by a wooden door and produced a key to the padlock that fastened it.

The house was one room with a courtyard of a kind at the back which was shared by others, yet enclosed by a high fence. The mud walls were plastered with newspapers, mostly advertisements of one kind or another, and the roof was the sheet of tin that comprised the roof of the whole

row of houses. One side of the room was taken up with a bed.
It was rope but had a mattress of a kind, covered by rough
sheets and a brightly-coloured blanket. To Esther, who had
slept on a straw mat on the floor every night, it looked very
fine. But it was the only fine thing in the house. The floor
was cow-dung, but not carefully swept as it had been in
Esther's house, but covered in dirt, husks, lime skins, and
all the litter of living. There was a table of sorts, stained
with all the drinks that had been spilt on it, and two rough
wooden benches. An old orange-box held the glasses and
bottles of drink. In the far corner was a rough fireplace and
some grimy utensils. Hanging up at the end of the bed were
a number of dresses such as the one the girl wore.

Esther stood humbly while Sidara flung off her shawl, and
took some perfume from a bottle. When she had rubbed
this into her skin, she said abruptly to Esther:

"Well? Do you think working for me better than returning
to your people and marrying?"

She saw Esther's hesitation and smiled briefly.

"You may cook and keep the house clean. That is all I am
asking: that, and a still tongue in your head."

"I will do that for you," Esther answered then, although
shame rose in her at the prospect of living among this
company.

"Then begin by boiling coffee," Sidara said and took down
a tin where a few coffee beans were.

By now the sky was darkening. Sidara's house was lit by
oil lamps and she sat by the door in the light of these, while
Esther, her head spinning with tiredness, kindled a fire and
began to wash the beans.

Presently a man came in and then others. They drank and
took no notice of Esther roasting, grinding, and then boiling the coffee, but one of them took a cup when she offered
it, and Sidara drank several cups. Esther served those who
desired it, and then suddenly felt their eyes upon her, consideringly. Sidara noticed it too and, frowning, jerked her

head towards the courtyard. Esther bowed her head and
crept out. There, against the wall, she found a kind of roof,
built perhaps to keep the wood dry in the rains. Here, she
lay down, hungry, but not knowing where to find food,
wrapped herself in her shawl, and at last fell asleep.

It said much for her tiredness and her youth that she slept
undisturbed until the morning in that place of unease and
noise, but certain it was that, when Sidara shook her
shoulder the next day, the daylight was already lighting
her dingy surroundings. She went to get water, following the
other women down the unfamiliar path to the springs. She
was very hungry, and the dawn was lighting the tree-tops
with a golden light. She thought of her home and momen-
tarily tears stung her eyelids but she blinked them angrily
away. She had no home. She seemed to be walking in a
nightmare, from which she would presently wake to find
herself beside Tara in her house, seeing her mother blowing
up the reluctant tinders for the morning coffee. The other
women called to one another, obviously well acquainted,
but none accosted her. She waited her turn at the water in
silence and then began the journey back. She felt faint with
lack of food, but Sidara, who had gone to bed, when she
returned, threw her some money and told her to buy bread
for their breakfast.

So began her life with Sidara. She found it hard work, even
though the house was small. She received no wages, but
was given enough to eat. Sidara gave her an old dress of
hers, and this, and the shawl given her by the trader, was
her only clothing. She had no shoes. She slept at night out
under the lean-to in the courtyard, sent out there as soon as
she had served the men that gathered evening by evening.
Once, frozen and unable to sleep, she had crept back into
the house late at night. But the man lying with Sidara had
heard her and caught her arm as she slipped in, with a
coarse jest, and she had fled in fright. Next day, Sidara had
slapped her angrily, and since then she had not ventured

within the house at night. She fetched water, swept the house, kindled the fire, and cooked what Sidara wanted. She bargained in the town, where she mingled with the other poor, and waited for the shop-keeper's attention while others were served before her. She washed Sidara's dresses and begged the use of an iron to iron them. She washed endless glasses and learned how to make the local spirit. Sidara was kind to her in a rough sort of way. Half the time she was hardly conscious whether Esther was there or not, though she was quick to be sharp if the work was not done. And Esther, in those days, was too tired often to do more than what she was told to do and, when she could, to sleep, for constant late nights made her always tired.

Once one of Sidara's friends had called when Sidara was out in the town and she sat for a while, watching Esther pounding the grain. She said suddenly:

"Why don't you go back to your home now?"

Esther had stopped, startled. She did not often think of home these days. She said nothing and the woman added, "If you stay here, you will become as one of us."

This had been said to Esther before and she answered with her eyes on the ground.

"I am a servant. My mistress asks nothing of me but the work of the house."

"Now, perhaps," the woman said not unkindly. "But it cannot always be so. Why do you not return to your own people?"

But this, Esther would not answer. She hardly knew herself, but within her was a bitterness she could not express towards those who had thrust her out into the unknown with so little respect for her wishes. She was afraid to return—who knew what story had reached them about her flight?—but another part of her did not want to. The woman sighed. "Later, you will be sorry," she said, and left.

Esther returned to her pounding, a set expression on her face. Until she knew where else she could live, she would stay where she could at least eat and sleep.

It was about a fortnight later that it happened. She had
been more and more conscious of the looks of the men whom
she served in the evening, and had hastened to finish her
duties and leave them, but, curiously, Sidara no longer
seemed to mind if the men spoke to Esther and jested with
her. Esther hardly ever listened to such jests and never
replied, but when things were spoken near her which she
could no longer ignore, she blushed and tried to turn away.
One evening Sidara said suddenly,

"I have an old dress I have finished with, which you may
have if you wish."

Esther took the one offered with the conventional expression
of thanks and was about to put it by, when Sidara said
sharply,

"I gave it to you to wear. Put it on. I want you to look
nice tonight."

Esther's expression did not change, but her heart beat
suddenly fast. Nevertheless she put on the dress. It was
blue and lower in the neck than she had worn. She pulled
her shawl around her before going into the house that
evening, but Sidara laughingly pulled it from her. "You
have no need of a shawl in this warm room," she said.
"Come here and show yourself!" She took her by the arm
and forced her into the centre of the small house.

"Well?" she demanded of the men who were gathered
there, with rather a forced laugh. "I've hired a house along
the street for anyone who wishes to use it."

Esther found her voice. "I . . . I will not," she gasped, but it
was a frightened, breathless voice and apparently only
added to her desirability, for several of the men laughed
kindly and considered her more carefully. She grew both
hot and confused as she heard money mentioned in low
tones. She was being sold! Hired out for the night to the
highest bidder! She looked in horror from one to the other,
but the house was growing dark and no one seemed to care
that the centre of attraction was so unwilling to play her part.

Finally, one man arose. Tall and young, he would have been handsome in other circumstances. Sidara, who had not released her grip on Esther's arm, seemed pleased and presently led the little servant out. Outside, Esther gasped in the fresh air and would have fallen on her knees.

"Lady, I can't! I won't! You promised I should not!" she said.

"Don't be foolish!" Sidara said roughly, but kindly enough. "You can't go on living here for nothing. There's much to enjoy in the life if you are careful. This man is kind and considerate. There is nothing to fear."

Nothing except the loss of her chastity; nothing except the shame to her person; nothing except the loss of the last shred of human dignity left to her.

"I will not!" Esther said again, desperate. Sidara lost her patience and shook her hard. "You'll do as you're told!" she hissed, her voice having to be lowered because of the men in the house. "Are you so much better than all of us that you think you can live without paying for it? Do you think you can run off from here, as you ran from your home? I tell you, you are well known already. No other way of life is open to you. You'll do as I bid you or you'll suffer for it. I'll see no one else will take you in. Now, will you go with your master, or shall I beat you into it?"

She seemed perfectly ready to do this, having seized a stick in her hand, but this made little impression on Esther. What else could she do? Where could she go? She remembered with fear that night on the hillside when she had first run away. She would not face that again, even if she could, and looking about her at the small fenced-in courtyard and hearing the noises in the other houses nearby: the chink of glasses, the blare of music and laughter of men, she felt caged and helpless. Sidara sensed, rather than saw, her defeat, and sounded satisfied as she said,

"There's a sensible girl. We'll have to get someone else to help in the house now two of us are working."

4 · *Learning*

LORD, *as I turn my mind to search for Thee,*
And as I daily study, question, sift,
Oh, let Thy Holy Spirit guard my questing soul
And keep it from the proud and sinful drift
Of thinking that my intellect can reach
Those mighty lessons that Thy Word doth teach.

"WE'RE HERE, HELEN, really here at last!" My room mate did a series of pirouettes around the room and stopped in front of me. "Do cheer up!" she urged. "It can't be as bad as all that!"

"Can't it?" I said sourly. (I had met her previously.) "How can you be so sure?"

"Well, I've been wanting to be here for years," she said. "Just one step from here to Burma!"

"That's true," I thought, stepping over my case and going to the window. "One step from here to my goal. But what a step and what a goal!"

Thus, my first night in a missionary training college.

Among those who enter a Bible training college will surely be found two extremists. On the one hand is the student for whom this represents a glorious opportunity, who has the idea that to live in such a fellowship, with unlimited opportunities for studying the Bible, is going to be the closest to heaven on earth that we are likely to achieve. On the other is the student who goes there as a necessary means to an end, unwillingly, and rather scornfully, with the 'I'll show them' attitude. Of course, I will add that in between these two extremes are what are, I trust, the majority of students, those who enter calmly, aware of what they are going to and ready to take the best from it. However, I arrived at my Bible college defiant, and as prickly as a hedgehog, ready to fight to the bitter end before submitting to a system which was still named the 'sausage machine'.

I was instantly aware of two things within my first fortnight. One was that although I was prepared for battle, there was no enemy. The only weapons used against me were prayer (which I did not see) and a loving concern to make a fighter for God on the mission field (of which I was not aware). The other thing was that I had suddenly become much cleverer than I had thought. There were only two graduates amongst that group of students and we were regarded as particularly clever. I mention this because it is a regrettable fact in the Christian world, that too often there is a reverence for degrees, which after all mean little, and mean nothing toward the spiritual worth of the person concerned. From being a positively mediocre person among your colleagues in the University, and then from being nothing special in the staff room, where they are all like you anyway, there comes this false elevation of 'giving God thanks for the great gifts which you have been given', and a quite unnecessarily frequent use of the verse, 'To whom much is given, of him much shall be required'. This has the twin effects of making you despise those who have such false values, and making you almost believe that you are a genius after all.

On my first evening, I was desperately unhappy, missing my friends of the staff room and others whom it had cost me dear to leave, and bitterly resenting the very atmosphere of quiet and peace around me. To make it worse we had 'duties' explained to us. It did not concern me for the moment, but it did my room mate. She was missing from 9.30 to 10 pm that evening and when she came back, she was red from suppressed laughter. She told me that she had been instructed in the art of a certain duty which involved preparing the bedrooms of the staff for night: turning back beds, folding bed-covers (just along the creases), drawing

curtains, filling hot-water bottles, and preparing trays for
morning tea. She—bless her!—thought it excruciatingly
funny. I did not. These women's institutions!

But there was something else which for the moment swept
me along with it: the glorious revelation of the opening
Bible. I had been starved of the Word. I had had a diet of
'Search the Scriptures' too long. Now there were tutors
who opened the Word, expounded it carefully, opened up
unexplored vistas of truth and wonder. For part of my course
there happened that year to be only two of us in the class.
To me, used to lectures of anything up to two hundred, it
could not seem else but strange, but I presently ceased to
think about the lack of students and gave my attention to
the teacher, who laid in my eager hands a wealth of hitherto
unknown material. I had paid scant attention to the Old
Testament previously, but now my heart leapt in response
to the plea of prophet after prophet to God's people: to the
mighty condemnations of Amos, to the heart-cry of Hosea.
I gazed in awe at the unfolding plan of God in Jewish
history as details were filled in. I was abysmally ignorant,
but no lack of knowledge surprised this teacher; no question
was too trivial to be carefully answered. From her, I gained
a love for the Old Testament which has never left me and
which I have since sought, on every occasion offered me, to
pass on to others.

Yet little things continued to nag at me: lights out at ten
thirty, set 'study hours' (as if I needed to have my study
organised for me!), household duties: one teaspoon here—
not those table mats, the others—one sheet fortnightly to the
laundry—do you have to be late for meals?—you must
attend student prayers. Waiting on table under the eye of
the house-keeper was quite and utterly infuriating: take one
plate at a time—set it down gently—serve from the left.
Have I joined up with a missionary society to be taught
this? What I chiefly found difficult was serving the staff.
Where I did things in the house for those who in turn did

the same things for me, then I thought it was fair and did not object. But when I was compelled to take a tray of breakfast, or to fill a hot-water bottle for a member of staff, then my pride rose up and I found it hard not simply to refuse. I suppose I had too recently been an inmate of the staff-room myself. I remember particularly one instance. On a Wednesday it was the custom to have afternoon tea. The four members of staff had it served in their common room, the students in ours. It fell to us all in turn, to have the job of preparing this tea. It meant setting out the cups and saucers in the common room in a certain way, cutting the bread, and so on. All perfectly ordinary jobs and as, on the whole, the job was done in an empty common room, I did not unduly object to the early part of the job, but after tea I had to wash up for the students, again free of objection, but then knock on the staff-room door, ask for permission to clear and take the tea things away on trays to wash, while the staff still sat around and talked. Nothing, you say, and how rightly! But, to me, it was humiliation complete. "I didn't come here to learn how to be a maid!" The first time it fell to my lot, I rebelled, firmly and conclusively, and when the washing-up of the students' things was finished, I returned to my books in the library. I always remember the girl who came to me there. She was an older student with whom I had little in common but who had (though heaven knows, I did nothing to deserve it) become very fond of me. She urged and persuaded for the best part of half an hour: not with sanctimonious arguments, but with a simple desire to see the job done.

"Why?" she kept asking, and although I knew the answer, I could not bring myself to put it into words, for the words would have been: "I am too proud." I think, though I didn't give her credit for it then, that she understood what I was feeling. At last, more to be rid of her than anything else, for I could not bring myself to be rude to her, I seized a tray, thundered on the staff-room door and

marched in, in a flaming temper without waiting for a
reply. They looked startled, as well they might. The Principal suggested that I 'left the door there' and a younger
member of staff got up to help me load the tray. My temper
carried me through the job in a stony silence, but no word of
rebuke was offered nor was any reference made to it later.
But for me, for some reason, that particular difficulty was
gone and I never had to struggle with myself over it
again.

One of the troubles was that I resented being disturbed
from my work. Once started, I wanted to go on, and I had
a full timetable. Then we would have gardening, and I
would have to go and prod unenthusiastically at the garden
with a fork; or 'singing' (shades of school days here. I'm
only surprised we never had gym) and I would have to
put down my essay, lose my line of thought, and obey the
bell. I remember the senior student of my first year: the
kind of girl that managed to make me feel just about as
inferior as the kitchen boy in the monastery of St Benedict,
coming to me after a singing class and asking me how I
could 'explain' my behaviour. "Stay after school a moment,
Brenda. I wish to speak to you." I exploded, verbally
anyway. But it was like hitting a child. Angrily, I went
along to her room later that night. Opening the door, I
found her trying to work with red eyes (she wasn't very
clever anyway). She looked at me. "I'm sorry," she said,
before I could get my apology started. "I really am." She
was apologising to me! I wished the world would stop
swinging around me!

There was a system called 'Bible Diploma': an exam every
Friday night on one or several books of the Bible. The
exam was an internal one and meant little, but the reading
for them was continually exciting. We, with our little
booklets and our S.U.! Don't let me run these down. They
are splendid in their place, but as you grow in the Christian
life, so grow away from these and read the Bible: read a

whole book, read the story of Jeremiah at a sitting, and you will enter as never before the agony of that prophet who was made 'a defenced city, an iron pillar' before God. The Sword of the Spirit, which is the Word of God.

Going to lectures that I did not want to go to was another labour. There was one that took place once a week in the evenings. It lasted for two hours. I could not but feel one first-class book on the subject concerned would have done us more good, but I could not really judge, for my only notebook for those lectures was a notecase of letters that needed to be written and a desk at the back of the room. Outwardly, I was beginning to conform: inwardly, I went my own way as far as I could. I was not wholly surprised to get a letter of warning from the society, after my first year in college; a warning on the question of discipline.

The Wycliffe Language Course that I attended between my two years at college was like a breath of fresh air. Little things sank down and bigger things came to the fore. The work was fun and the fellowship invigorating. We seemed to catch the first whiff of the mission field. Crowded accommodation, washing under freezing cold-water taps, classes in army-type huts with shaky tables, all these things were nothing to us. We worked hard in class but learnt from one another as well as from the instructors. Mid-morning, a bell would bring us together in 'Chapel-Marquee'. Often there I would look around me at the other students. There was Hilda, well clear of thirty, small, and finding the course very difficult, but sturdily plodding on. An ex-parish worker, she had been called to the mission field by an address she gave herself to her young people. She was due to sail in a few weeks for India. Or big Stan Brittain, missionary from Liberia, who spoke to us once on 'missionary casualties'. I have never forgotten his description of how his station was found to be the centre of leprosy infection. Even his only child was suspect. "It drove me to

my knees," he said, and something in his voice stilled us all,
"and when I was there I realised my position was an unfamiliar one." That humble confession made a profound
impression on me. What a warning it was! If he had thus
fallen, how would I fare in this warfare of flesh against
spirit!

There was Erica, interpreter in a German Government
department for many years: Mini, who had spent the years
of the war in a concentration camp: Wilfred, escaper from
East Berlin: Ron, with travels and experiences of all sorts
behind him. Then there were others, less striking perhaps,
but with the same purpose: Paddy, a quiet-voiced little
suburban librarian, a girl who may be patterned in a
hundred libraries, yet a girl 'set apart', consecrated for the
Master's use; Edwin, a round-faced, ruddy farmer's son
with a broad Devonshire accent. His father's farm would
pass to his brother-in-law and Edwin had his sights set far
beyond the green lanes of Devon. And so we gathered, for
a short time united, before being flung by the mighty hand
of God into the farthest corners of the earth. Why? What
distinguishing marks do we bear to join this great profession? Why me? was often an unspoken whisper in those
days. Why, indeed? An unanswered question; we are but
part of the army of weakness conscripted to confound the
strong in the might of the Beloved.

". . . for ye see your calling, brethren, how that not many
wise men after the flesh, not many mighty, not many noble,
are called: but God hath chosen the foolish things of the
world to confound the wise; and God hath chosen the
weak things of the world to confound the things which are
mighty."

The Language Course drew to its close. Few addresses
were exchanged. Our one sure meeting-place had no
address. For the last time a hundred and fifty young voices
filled the Chapel-Marquee and rolled away down the
country-side:

"My heart is resting, O my God,
 I will give thanks and sing:"

Yes, that was it: thanksgiving. What else could we give
when God had so greatly blessed us over the past weeks?

"My heart is at the secret source
 Of every precious thing."

Pat, Kenneth, Janet, Elizabeth, Michael . . . vessels for
His use. Wherever, whenever He may use us. This is our
sure confidence and our desire.

"Thou art my portion, saith my soul,
 Ten thousand voices say,
 The music of their glad 'Amen!'
 Will never fade away."

The music of their glad 'Amen!' will never fade away.
Someone said of 'Camp Wycliffe' that it either makes you
or breaks you. Things were not miraculously changed, as I
entered my second college year, but certainly they were
better. My six weeks at Wycliffe had refocused the whole
picture.
A sense of proportion. That's what often disappears in a
missionary training college. That is why one of my greatest
battles concerned the question of wearing a hat to church.
That is why I saw girls in tears because they could not pass
their Bible Diploma exams. Proportion. "Co-operate in
your own humiliation." That's what we were told in one of
the addresses in Wycliffe. How my proud spirit cringed at
that. Translate it in training into simply doing what you
are told instead of resisting and fighting to the last stand
on things which are unimportant. Save your energies for
the forces of Satan. The things that cause us to stumble are
often so very small. So small: yet the devil seizes on them
and fills our minds with them. We are so absorbed in what
we consider to be other people's pettiness that we entirely

fail to see that in getting so worked up about it, we are
failing into exactly the same error ourselves. I don't really
think for one minute that there are petty little restrictions and rules just in order to teach one how to cope with
them, but certainly such can be used of the Lord to show
up our latent pride, to force us to realise that many of
our objections to doing things are based on the argument
that they make us feel small and look small. If that is so,
then we haven't yet realised that we *are* small . . . "but, as
for me, I am a worm and no man".

Let me relate one incident here that took place shortly
after I left Bible College. I was an officer at a big mixed
teenage house-party. One of my jobs, one day, was to
supervise the team of youngsters laying the tables for about
a hundred and fifty people. Directly after the midday meal,
one of the leaders of the house-party came to me and said
quite angrily, and exceedingly publicly:

"Helen, I wish you'd learn to lay a table. Every child
[there were about seven or eight children, belonging to
officers] should have *two* teaspoons provided, not one!"

Later in the day, another officer (a University student)
said to me: "Helen, however did you manage to keep your
temper over those teaspoons? I was boiling!"

I looked at her in surprise, for I had quite forgotten the
incident, and then said, without thinking,

"But was it worth being angry? Over teaspoons?"

That was something I had learnt from my Bible college!
I worked hard, that second year, for apart from my set
studies, I had taken on a part-time job to help pay my fees.
But although I was happier within the college than I had
been previously, I still experienced no real joy at the thought
of my future: in fact, in times of depression, I often would
ask God, beg Him, to take away His call from me.

Then one day, a friend of mine, a candidate of another
mission, fell downstairs. It was discovered, some months
later, that this had caused a detached retina and had tem-

porarily damaged her sight. It was thought at the time that she would, because of this, not be able to go abroad. About that time I was engaged in one of my usual self-pitying wails to God about having to be a missionary. Then I read the verse in Malachi, which says: "Ye have wearied the Lord with your words." And suddenly, into my mind, came the thought of Mary, who, we thought then, had been stopped from going abroad so abruptly, and the Lord spoke quite plainly to me, saying: "Be careful how you pray lest I give you your request. I could prevent you going abroad without so much as lifting my little finger, if that is what you really want." Horrified, I jumped up from my knees. He should not take His Best from me! I did not want that! From that day forward, I never again prayed that God would take His calling from me.

As the second year drew to its close, I found that, much as I loved my present companions, I was beginning to look on from them, away towards the yet untried pastures of the mission field. The friends of those days are friends yet, for with them and because of them, I learned much: and when they finally saw me leave, I was as ready, anyway, as they could make me, for the path that lay before.

*

ESTHER HAD ENTERED THE COFFEE HOUSE that was down the street from Sidara's house, to beg the loan of some glasses. The owner, who knew her, had gone to fetch them and Esther leant against the counter, waiting. Standing there, she became aware of three men in conversation at one of the tables. She would not have noticed them except that one of them was a stranger and, presumably imagining her to be in the employ of the house, signed for her to take his cup. She went forward and took it, since the owner had not returned, and, refilling it, put it again before him.

He was speaking, and his two companions were listening

politely to him. Esther heard the words:

"It does not matter where you are, or who you are, you may pray to God Himself without the need of any saints to intercede for you."

"Don't you believe in the saints?" asked one of his listeners. "I believe that they were holy men and that we can learn a lot from them," was the man's answer. "But I do not find anywhere in this book that we need them to pray to God for us. It says here, that there is but one mediator between God and man, the man Christ Jesus." Saying this, he brought out the book he had been holding on his knee and opened it. Esther felt the blood rush to her face. Time flew back for her and she was once again standing before Joseph's father, holding in her hand the precious book. And prayer . . . when had she last heard anyone speak about prayer? She remembered crouching under a rock and praying that God would send her travellers to take her out of the night's dangers. He had done so, but had she ever spoken to Him again?

The two men sitting with the speaker were now obviously in disagreement with him.

"We have many other books besides the one you hold," one was saying. "Are we to disbelieve them?"

"Whether you believe them or disbelieve them is not my business," the man said quietly. "In as far as they record lives and deeds of holy men I think they can be a blessing to us. But I believe that this book—this book only," he repeated gently, "is the Word of God."

There was a chorus of shocked disagreement. "You do not teach the truth!" said one of the men, rising in anger. "We will not listen. Come, brother." He put a hand on his companion's shoulder and they both left the house.

Still the house-owner had not returned. Esther gathered her courage.

"Sir, if you please," she said.

The man had been sitting with his head bent over his book,

but he now looked up at her. His expression did not change, but Esther knew that he knew who and what she was. She was dressed now as Sidara had been when she first saw her: her eyes were shadowed, her lips painted. And now that she had spoken, she did not know what to say. How could she, a woman of the streets, say that she wanted to hear more about this book, that she wanted to learn to read it? How could the name of the one she had been taught was holy and without sin, pass her defile? lips? So she was silent, and hung her head.

"What is it?" the man asked her. "Did you want to ask me a question?"

"It . . . it was about the book . . ." Esther began very timidly. "Could you . . ."

But she was interrupted by the owner, who had at last returned with a dozen glasses.

"Now then girl, what's this? You don't ply your trade in my house. This is a respectable bar, not a brothel," he said roughly. "Take these and be off with you. You should know better than to talk with my customers. Go along with you!" and he thrust the glasses into her hands and hustled her out of the door before the other man could intervene. Then he came back.

"I'm sorry about that, sir," he said. "You won't want to be troubled with that sort of woman, you being a preacher and a learned man. Impudent little hussy!"

"She is not in your employ, then?" asked the man.

"She is not," the owner answered indignantly. "I don't go in for that kind of thing here."

"She had not asked me anything," the other said quietly. "I think she was not thinking of me—perhaps about something I was saying a moment ago. Who is she?"

"If you mean, what is her name, I don't know," responded the man, beginning to stack the dirty cups and glasses. "They're all the same to me. She has a room on the main road, opposite the cloth shop of the Arabs."

"Has she been doing this long," asked the preacher.

"I don't know," said the man crossly. "There was a story that she was left destitute in the town, having travelled from the plateau country with some traders who would take her no farther."

"How long ago would that be?" pursued the enquirer, and this time he brought a note out of his pocket and played with it on the table.

The bar-owner's manner became slightly more mellow. "It was over two years past," he said. "For a time she worked for a woman named Sidara as a servant, but it is said from this rains she has been free for what a man will pay for her."

"Hmmm," the man pondered. Then he rose and with a word of farewell, leaving the note on the table, he left.

Sidara was expecting a baby. She was out of reason angry at this and hardly ever left the house. Although she had spoken first of getting someone else to do the housework, she had done nothing and Esther had continued to serve her, bearing with her ill-temper as best she might. Esther, these days, was weary and uncaring. She had sometimes thought of taking poison and thus ending a life which she had no desire to prolong; once she had bought some powder from a passing trader, but had been afraid to use it and thrown it away. She ate enough and dressed well, for Sidara was angry if she did not. At night, she went with the man who desired her and said and did the right things with a mechanical grace. Sidara sometimes wondered sharply why any man should desire so cold a companion, but because Esther was young, and because there always clung to her an appealing kind of wistfulness and beauty, she did not lack customers. The money was paid to Sidara who dressed and fed Esther but gave her little more. Esther did not even ask what the amount was, and when others took her aside and whispered that it was time she left Sidara and set up on her own account, she only answered, "Why should I care?" It seemed that all feeling and passion had burnt out that first terrible night of shame and misery, and that there was a wall around her heart that nothing could break down: nothing, that is, until this day; until she had seen again that treasure: the Word of God.

Now, as she sat in the sun, picking over the grains of wheat before her, to separate the husks from the corn, her mind was living again in those former days, and she remembered with a rush of pain and remorse the words, "Jesus said, I will be with you always."

"Will you be all day over that?" came Sidara's impatient call from within the house.

"I have nearly finished," Esther said, without losing her train of thought. As she spoke, a shadow fell across the dish at her feet. Startled, she looked up and saw the man of the morning's encounter looking kindly down at her.

"May God give you health," he said formally and she replied, rising to her feet and staring at him.

"You were about to speak to me this morning," he went on. "What would you have said?"

"It was the book," Esther said. "I wanted you to read me something."

"What do you know of that book?" he asked her and she saw for the first time that he was holding it.

"I—I know it is the Word of God," she answered. "And that it tells of the one who is the Saviour of the world."

"And is that one your Saviour too?"

She looked up at him, puzzled. "I don't know what you mean," she said. "You—you see, I know so little and I cannot read to know more, although I have a book."

"What book have you?" he asked. "May I see it?"

"Yes, I will fetch it." Esther ran into the house, to the little box which held her clothes and possessions, such as they were, but Sidara caught her arm.

"Who are you talking to, little idler?" she demanded, "and

why have you left the grain for the goats and the birds to eat?"

"It is a man I met this morning," Esther answered submissively. "He wishes to speak with me."

"I have never seen him before. Where is he from?"

"I don't know. He is a preacher of the Word of God."

"What does that mean? A priest?"

"I don't know," Esther pulled away from her. "Let me go. Is not his money as good as another's?"

She was released, albeit reluctantly, and ran to get that little book that she had not looked upon for many months. When she went back to the street, the man looked at the book and smiled.

"You will find the stories of the Saviour in here," he told her. "Shall I read one to you?"

"I—I—" stammered Esther, glancing at the dark doorway.

"We cannot talk here," the man said, realising her thought. "Will you come and talk elsewhere?"

"Do you know, sir," Esther said hesitantly, "what men will say if you go off with me?"

The man laughed. "The same, I expect, as they said of our Lord when He intervened to save a woman taken in adultery," he said. "It is no matter. Come."

They went, she following him, along the street and a little way out of the town, until they reached a stone ledge that marked a river. Here he sat and she stood before him but would not sit too.

After a moment, when he had sat with his head bowed as if in thought, he looked up and smiled at her.

"What is your name?" he asked her.

"Esther, sir," she replied.

"Well, Esther, will you tell me when and where you heard of the Saviour of the world?"

It was an unexpected question and the girl felt the blood rush to her cheeks. It had been so long since she had thought of the past and the home that once had been hers. And she had never spoken of it to anyone, and here was a complete stranger asking her to tell him, as if it was the most normal thing in the world.

"It was—at my home, sir," she said at last, hanging her head. "There was a preacher there—they called him the 'Evangelist', who often gathered neighbours to him and children too, and he would tell us stories about—about Jesus."

"Will you tell me why you left your home?" asked the preacher gently.

There was a long pause and then Esther answered slowly, "I—I don't think I can, sir. I do not want to think about it. I have never spoken of it. It is not my home any longer. My home is here."

"And your work is here?"

"There was nothing I could do," Esther said, ashamed before his kindly gaze.

He nodded. "You spoke of Jesus as the Saviour of the world," he said then. "Do you know that He is interested in you, just you, as well?"

She frowned in puzzlement, and he went on,

"Will you listen to a story, Esther? The story told in this book that you so much want to read?"

She did not answer but she raised her head and her eyes answered for her.

"When God first made the world," began the preacher slowly, wanting her to follow every word, "He made it a beautiful place and He made a man and a woman to live in it. But instead of just being happy and doing what God wanted them to in that lovely place, this man and woman disobeyed God. And the men and women who were born after them also chose their own way, rather than His. And today people are still doing it. This book says," and he opened it and read, "Everyone has sinned and fallen short of the glory of God". He paused, wondering if she understood, but Esther made no comment. "Now God is a holy

God," went on the man, "and He cannot let sinners come to Him unless they pay the penalty for their sin and so are forgiven. Just as light and darkness cannot be in the same place so God and sin cannot be together. We read here that the penalty of sin is death. Now you know a little about the Lord Jesus. Do you know what happened to Him?"

"He was crucified," she answered.

"Do you think He deserved to be crucified? Was He a robber, or a murderer?"

She shook her head.

"That's right. He was none of those things. You see God, even though we were sinners, loved us and wanted to be able to forgive us, so He sent His Son, the Lord Jesus Christ, whom we now call the Saviour of the world, to die in place of us and to pay the penalty for our sins. And because He was His Son, and because He was quite without sin, God accepted His death, in place of ours. So because He paid this penalty, we can be forgiven our sin and become a friend to God and be able to talk with Him, and when we die in this life we can go to Him in Heaven. Now let me read you something out of your book."

He opened the little book and read very slowly:

"For God so loved the world, that He gave His only begotten Son that whosoever believeth in Him should not perish but have everlasting life."

He took a pen from his pocket and carefully underlined the words.

"Whoever we are, whatever we've done, if we believe in Jesus and want to follow Him in the way that He will show us, then because of His death on the cross, we will be forgiven our sin and will be new people and find a new life with Him."

There was a long pause. When at last the man looked up, he saw tears in Esther's eyes.

"I could never find that new life, sir," she whispered. "Not one such as I am. I have sinned so much. I shall never be a friend of God. There is no hope for me in what you have said."

The preacher smiled. "Let me tell you one more story and then I have done," he said. "This is a story that the Lord Jesus Himself told. Once, there were two men who went to a church to pray: one was a very holy man—like a priest— and he prayed like this: 'Lord, thank you for not making me a sinner like others. I am always fasting and I give you money and come always to church.' But the other man there, a man whose whole life had been evil, whose work was that which made him hated by everyone, prayed: 'Lord, be merciful to me, a sinner!' Now, said Jesus, which of these two had his prayer heard by God? It was the one who had sinned, but who knew he had sinned and so asked forgiveness. He was the one God delighted in. For there is nothing so lovely to God as a sinner who comes to Him and believes in His mercy."

"How may I believe?" Esther said timidly, after a moment's thought.

"By first being sorry for your sin. Do you know what repentance is, my child?"

She shook her head.

"It is being sorry for your sin, and determining to try not to sin again."

"But—but my work is sin," she faltered.

"Yes, you would have to leave it behind you; it is true."

"But I cannot do that," Esther said. "My mistress would not let me."

"The perhaps you should leave your mistress," the man said gently.

"But I have nowhere else to go. There is no other place."

"For that, you must trust God to show you where to go."

"How could God do that?"

"Have you never heard of prayer, child?"

She was silent. Her mind was back on that black hillside.

"Once I prayed," she said, "but then I was not as I am now."

"If you pray now, He will hear you just the same," was the reply. "Come now, let us together ask the Lord to help you to know how you may leave this work of yours."

"But—I am promised tonight. I dare not refuse."

"Good," he said unexpectedly, and smiled at her. "For now you will early see the power of God working. Come closer to me and we will pray together."

He held out his hand and she took it and came near him. The road was deserted. The preacher closed his eyes and bowed his head.

"Dear Father," he prayed, "you see this child of yours desiring to believe in you and yet held fast by the chains of the life she is leading. Deliver her tonight from the sin that she would commit that she may learn to trust in you for the future. We ask it for your glory. Amen."

Then he rose to his feet with happiness and confidence in his eyes and voice. "Now," he said, "you will see the Lord work for you tonight, and when He has done that, then ask Him to show you how to leave your mistress without anger. And when He has answered that prayer, then come to me and we will talk again." He let go her hand and putting back into it her precious little book, he strode away.

Sidara was bad-tempered when she returned, but Esther's mind was full of what she had heard, so she did not greatly heed the complaint that the lunch had been kept waiting, and merely blew up the fire ready to heat the spiced lentils.

"What has that man been talking to you about?" Sidara demanded presently, seeing her abstraction.

"He is a preacher," Esther said, "and he read from his book to me and read a little from my book too."

"What book have you?"

Esther hesitated for a moment but then drew out the book and handed it to Sidara who looked at it curiously.

"I didn't know you had this. Where did you get it?"

"I brought it with me," Esther said quietly and Sidara said no more. She had once or twice tried to question

Esther about her home and family, but had met with such stony silences that she had long since given up.

"What are these words here that are underlined?" she asked.

"They are what the preacher read to me," Esther told her. "I cannot read them but they say that God sent His Son to die for us to help us find a new life." She rose from the fire, set the food before Sidara and held out a basin for her to wash her hands. Sidara put the book down and did so, looking curiously up into the face of the young girl.

"You did not tell me you thought of such things," she said.

"I know very little," was the quiet answer, "but I would like to know more."

The afternoon passed without further reference to the book or the preacher, and about five o'clock the men began to come in for the evening's drinking. Sidara reclined on the bed, propped up, so that her condition was not obvious, and kept up her usual lively flow of conversation, while Esther served them. Always Esther was watching the door waiting for the one she was expecting, but he did not come. Only a friend of his put his head round the door:

"Sidara! Halaku has been called to the city to answer a law case and won't come in tonight. He asked me to tell you."

Sidara nodded acknowledgement and Esther escaped from the room. A thrill swept through her body and she found she was trembling. Her first request! What had the preacher said? She had taken a jug of water as if to refill it and now she went into the little backyard, for it seemed easier to pray out there.

"Please God, let Sidara be willing for me to go," she said softly.

One by one the men went and Esther prepared for the night, washing up a few cups, and closing the shutters. Then she gathered her courage and went to Sidara who was lying half-asleep on the bed.

"May I ask you something?" she said.

"Why not?" Sidara said lazily.

"I want to stop working here and go away from the town."
There was a moment's silence. Esther bowed her head,
scarcely daring to breathe. Then Sidara sat up. She did not
seem angry: more puzzled.

"With this preacher?" she asked.

"No, not with him. I do not yet know where I shall go, or
what I shall do, but I know I want to go."

Sidara said nothing.

"I do not want to leave you in haste, or in anger," Esther
said, taking courage from this silence. "I can stay until you
find someone else to do your housework for you, if you like.
I have not forgotten that you housed me and fed me when
I was alone and homeless."

Sidara looked at her curiously. "And have you also not
forgotten," she thought, but did not say, "that I have made
you work for over two years without wages, that I forced
you to sell yourself and have given you nothing?" Aloud,
she said:

"Yesterday, the father of my child came and offered to take
me into his home. I had been meaning to tell you all day."
Esther's head lifted, blood pulsing through her body until
she felt almost faint.

"You mean you are going with him?" she said breathlessly.

"Yes, I am," Sidara answered. "So you see I will put
nothing in the way of your leaving." She smiled suddenly
and reached out her arms to the younger girl. "You have
been a good girl, Esther. May this new road lead you to
happiness!"

Esther stumbled down the dark, stony road to her own little
room. Around her were all the familiar noises of talk and
drinking. One or two men called to her but she did not
answer. Entering the little mud room, she pulled the door
shut, latched it and almost fell on the bed. Lying, her head
on her arms, she wondered at herself. She had found free-

dom, she could leave this place of evil remembrances, she had seen the power of God work on her behalf: but instead of joy, such a weight of sorrow filled her heart as she had never known. Suddenly, she began to cry and the more she tried to control herself, the more she wept. That hard wall she had erected around her heart was crumbling, that tight rein she had kept on her true feelings was relaxing, and for the first time her heart lay defenceless and open: and thus she met God. And she could say nothing; only, after a time, through the multitude of her increasing sobs, a listener, had there been one nearby, would have heard the words:

"Lord, be merciful to me, a sinner."

5 · *Shadows*

DEAR WORTHY LORD, *full preciously,*
Thou dost defend Thine own.
In this assault, we clearly see
A hand against the Throne.

And so our Hands are lifted up
Lest there be bitter loss:
Refusal, Saviour, of Thy Cup,
Denial of Thy Cross.

O turn the Powers of Calvary
On this imperilled soul,
Let him who is sore wounded be
By pierced Hands made whole.

AMY CARMICHAEL.*

A TALL, TERRACED HOUSE with a faded front door and an assortment of bells. I choose one that looks as if it might work. Presently the door opens and a warm smell of cabbage and over-worked drains hits me. The woman in a dirty dress, red-faced and with floury hands, stares at me.

A pause, and a smile (memory of college lectures), and, "Good afternoon. I'm one of the lady-workers from the parish church. I'm just calling down the street to get to know folk and see if there's anyone looking for a church to go to."

"Oh—well, we're—"

"'Oo is it, Mum?" This, sharply, from inside.

"A lady from the church."

A number of *sotto voce* sentences ensue: then,

* Quoted by permission of the Dohnavur Fellowship.

"Give 'er sixpence for whatever she's collecting for and come back and 'elp me!"

"Er—yes." The woman produces a greasy handbag and starts to fumble.

"But really—I don't want——" I begin, but a baby is starting to cry.

"Come *on*, Mum!"

"Oh, sorry, don't seem to 'ave any change," the harassed woman says. "Come back termorrow, will you, dearie?"

"But I——"

But the door is quietly and firmly shut and I am left, trying not to mind, on the doorstep.

It was not my idea that I spend some time in a parish after leaving Bible College, but the society thought it would be good for me to have some months there and thus find prayer support and gain experience of parish life.

I was warmly received into the fellowship of the parish and did not regret the time spent there. Much of my time was spent visiting, mostly in the poorer sections of the parish, and I was often struck dumb by what seemed to be the impassable barrier between myself and those I was trying to help. Here was I, English born and educated, not lacking in worldly comfort, and I was face to face with a West Indian mother, whose husband was in prison, and who was trying to care for four children, all under ten, in one room. And I had to tell her about the love of God. Good training, perhaps, for the mission field, but puzzling and hurtful at the time.

"What can *you* do for me?" said one young father." Can you find me work? Can you show me a home out of this filthy area? Can you bring my wife back?"

I knew the standard answer. I knew that if he came to Christ and learned to trust Him, He would help him to arrange his life and manage his family, but where could I find words that didn't sound facile and meaningless to tell him? In any case, the door was already shut.

Once or twice I went out with the London City Missionary who was attached to the same parish. It was the first time I had met one of these missionaries and I was very impressed. Few doors shut in his face and yet he was one of the most faithful preachers of the gospel I had ever known. Out his little Testament would come at door after door. Faced with the kind of desperation I have instanced above, he was not speechless but eager to show how Christ could help us in living our daily lives. It was a privilege to go with him and watch.

It was in this period—during, as it were, the final girding of my loins for the mission field—that the heaviest attack of Satan fell on me.

My lax attitude to doctrine quite horrified an Irish friend of mine at Bible College. I remember having an argument, more in a teasing spirit than anything else, with her one night on the question of the term 'altar' as opposed to 'communion table'. I maintained that since the Oxford dictionary's primary definition of the word 'altar' was 'communion table', the use of the former was quite permissible. It all meant very little to me, and, having fed the argument rather lazily for twenty minutes or so and watched my friend getting more and more excited, I was shocked when she burst into tears. I was repentant but surprised. I didn't know a matter as trivial as that could mean so much to anyone.

I had, furthermore, hardly read the basis of the society I had joined. I felt the Lord had called me to work in it; evidently they felt the same and I had not considered further. I know now, that my intellect had never fully been satisfied concerning the doctrines of Evangelical churchmen, because it had never been applied to them. And suddenly, I began to disbelieve the Bible.

I had happened to pick up some little books about other religions. The tone in which they were written was scornful: the writers implied that no one of sense would believe in

them. Their holy books were referred to: small sections
were quoted and mocked as having no meaning. Their
doctrines were paraded as ridiculous and misleading. Now
I have always had a tendency to support the under-dog and
the way these little booklets were written made me angry.
Instinctively I wanted to defend these religions, with their
huge followings, from these petty and spiteful remarks. I
began to consider how easy it would be to write such a book
about Christianity. Suppose such a verse as "And there was
a hole in the midst of the robe, as the hole of an habergeon,
with a band about the hole that it should not rend" was
isolated from its context and held up as the kind of thing
the Christian's Bible tells us about. How impossible the
doctrine of the atonement could be made to sound if
written about in the same way as the writers of these books
had written about Islam. If one, as it were, turned the heat
on Christianity, how much could be said against it. How
nonsensical would parts of the Bible sound if one were
determined to criticise it. This is how it began.

Few people appreciated the very real pit into which I
speedily sank during this period. Few could take it seriously
that a committed missionary candidate could have such
doubts. I know to one at least of my friends, it sounded
incredibly childish and silly. Up to that point, though I
had been a Christian for over ten years, I had never doubted
the facts of my salvation. Now, suddenly, my feet slipped
on that everlasting rock, and I looked appalled into that
morass of fear and uncertainty which looks so dark to those
who have once walked in the light. There, in the heart of
London, supported faithfully by those of my friends who
knew, the last, and victorious, battle was fought with the
Prince of Darkness to keep a missionary back from ever
reaching the field. At last I turned hungrily to those
doctrinal books I had hitherto scorned, and studied them
with a desperate desire to know and understand the main
tenets on which our faith was based. And, at length, tenta-

tively and ashamed, I stood once more, this time with a firmer grasp of the principles of my faith. I have heard people say sometimes, "I have a simple faith: I don't bother much with doctrine," and I wonder if they are not thus leaving a hole in their armour that Satan will delight— one day when they least expect it—to assail.

How quick is this Prince of Darkness to see the chink in the armour! How swift to attack in the place we least expect him to! How he fights for the souls of those in our future fields of service! How we need to take to us the whole armour of God: to rest our faith solidly and securely upon the Word of Life!

So the moment approached. It had been six years since my call and I could not believe my departure was really imminent. In me was a twofold feeling: one the knowledge that I must go on, for my own happiness and good, not only for my pride's sake; the other a shrinking with all my heart from the leave-taking this would mean, for I was very close to my parents and they had no other daughter.

There was, in those days, a 'Pre-sailing Conference' held for recruits. I never greatly favoured a gathering of missionaries, even young ones, and had already decided to be late for it. It was due to start on a Monday, the day which happened to follow the Harvest Festival at our church. It was easy to persuade myself that I was needed in the distribution of fruit and flowers throughout the parish and to ring up after lunch to explain I couldn't come until the next day. But, to my surprise, the Overseas Secretary, who answered the phone, had obviously had enough of me. He did not listen to my explanation, but simply told me firmly to get the 4.20 train from London and arrive in time for the first meeting. I was too surprised to refuse.

The conference was held in a beautiful place at a beautiful time of year, autumn. I wandered out and around as often as I could, just glorying in the colours and in the quietness. We had lectures and discussions: I have a notebook full of

them, but, as often with me, the main blessing was found
in that quiet communion with God in a place of surpassing
loveliness. I remember one tree that I often looked at in
those times. It stood among the others, which at this
season were clothed in bright beauty, but this tree had been
struck by lightning and was black and dead. Nevertheless it
was standing among the others: as high as they were and as
sturdy. And it appealed to me very much. I was going to
leave the beauty that I was accustomed to, the land that I
knew and loved, the parents and friends I leant on who made
life bright and happy for me, and I was going to be stripped
of all things that at present made life what it was, but I
was not going to fall; I was going to stand straight and
endure. I would not give in. And in His time, when the
years of apprenticeship were over, then the Lord may
choose again to invest me with love and beauty of a different
sort, in a different place. But until then, I would not give
way.

Inexorably, the wheels turned. I made some home-made
prayer-cards. I remember writing on some:

"My weakness: His strength.
My failure: His beginning.
My death: His life."

I have understood that a little since, although its full
meaning I have yet to learn. But I knew my weakness all
right in those weeks.

I had heard little about the pain of separation, from other
missionaries. I think we are probably only too anxious to
forget such an experience. Once on the field, there are
other things to think of and the pain of that first parting is
just filed away as something inevitable that all missionaries
must face. Friends did all they could for me then. Eight or
nine letters arrived every day assuring me of prayer,
reminding me that 'The Lord will undertake'. Yes, He
undertakes, for I am here today but the pain was not

lessened, the sorrow had to be borne. How thankful we should be that we do not see into the future. I never dreamed, as I looked down into my mother's tearful eyes as she tried to smile goodbye, that the next time I laid eyes on her she would be sunk in a coma and within four days of her death.

The journey—by plane—was brief: about twenty-two hours. I had flown a number of times before so had not the distraction of being excited at flying. I changed planes at Athens and found a brief thrill in seeing the Isles of Greece in bright moonlight. It was dawn when we neared my destination.

"We will be landing at our destination in one hour and ten minutes," announced the calm English voice of the captain.

"It's all right for you," I thought vehemently. "In a day or two you'll be right back where you came from."

"It is at present veiled in a cloud," added the speaker.

Cloud! I could have laughed. It was more than cloud. It was dank and deep depression.

As I descended from the plane I felt in a nightmare. I had an idiotic idea of running madly across the airfield, anywhere, as long as it wasn't into the airport building, anywhere as long as it wasn't to the prison reception desk! I handed over my passport and waved at the missionary who had come to meet me whom I vaguely recognised. We couldn't speak because of the distance. I hoped I didn't look as miserable as I felt.

"How long are you staying here?" asked the official who looked at my passport. I tried to speak and failed. Clearing my throat, I tried again. "I'm going to live here," I said. I did not see or hear his reaction to this. "I'm going to live here. I'm going to live here!" My words mocked me. My 'sentence' had begun.

*

IT WAS A LONG, LOW HOUSE, white-washed and glaring in
the sun, with a tin roof which reflected the day's burning
heat. Sleeping on a low chair, in the shade with her fat
chin sagging on her ample bosom, was the Lady Elizabeth.
Behind her, Esther stood, keeping the flies from the face of
her mistress with a big palm leaf. She had drawn up a small
rain-water barrel that had been standing nearby, and was
half-sitting on the edge of that. It was this that caught the
eye of Mistress Fonteye as she passed: "Stand up, girl!
What are you thinking of?" she hissed. "Are you to sit
when waiting on your mistress?"

Esther did not reply to the rebuke, apart from bowing her
head: and she rose at once to her feet: but her mouth was
slightly twisted and her eyes, kept lowered, were smouldering. Was this the new life God had offered her?

The morning after Sidara had agreed that she should go
from Mulata, Esther had had a long talk with the preacher.
They had prayed together, and afterwards the words of her
mother on her wedding morning, long since forgotten, had
come back to Esther, and she had decided to seek her aunt's
protection at Engadi. The preacher had found a friend of his
who could take her part of the way, for the journey was a
long one: the rest of the way, she had travelled in the
company of chance travellers. Finally, a day's journey from
Engadi, she had fallen in with two women who were
visiting Engadi because a relative of theirs had died nearby.
Engadi, Esther discovered, was only a short distance from a
very holy place where there was a famous church and a
monastery known throughout the whole country.

She had asked her two companions if they knew her aunt,
but they were strangers to the town. However, they kindly
offered to ask at the house where they were expected and
when they arrived, they led Esther first to this house.

"Mistress Hanna?" said someone. "Yes. I know her. She
works for the Lady Elizabeth in the big compound behind
the Church of the Three Marys. You will find her up there

in the kitchens. Anyone will guide you."

"Dear Lord, make her willing to receive me," Esther prayed inwardly as she walked slowly up the street.

Engadi was a small town, boasting only one or two shops and a small hotel. It was perched on the edge of an enormous cliff, and the greenery around was abundant and luxuriant. Dust rose under Esther's feet, and the sun beat warm upon her. She was a stranger and she pulled her shawl around her to hide her face as she walked. She reached the Church of the Three Marys at last, and timidly entering the compound, knelt to kiss the steps and stayed for a while in the cool shadows of the silent walls. There was nobody about. Then, a little quieter in soul, she went on. Immediately she saw the big compound, fenced in with a high fence of stone and brushwood. She could not see over the wall and the big gates looked formidable, so she went towards the back of the compound where surely there was another entrance for servants. Finding a smaller door, she knocked on the tin and, there being no immediate answer, walked in.

"What is it?" a voice demanded roughly and the watchman appeared from within a small hut by the gate.

"I seek my aunt, good master," Esther replied. "Mistress Hanna. They tell me to seek her here."

The man was mollified by the title and her respectful bow. "She works in the kitchen," he said. "Did she tell you to come here?"

"No. I have come from a far country in the hope that she can give me shelter," the girl answered.

"Come then."

The compound was vast, containing many houses. The big white-washed house in the centre was obviously the house of the mistress and it was around to the back of this that the watchman led Esther, to a long low building standing among trees. Smoke was issuing from this and it was obviously the kitchen.

"Wait," the watchman told Esther, and disappeared inside.

Now the moment had come, Esther was consumed with fears. What would her aunt be like? Would she be angry with her? What had she heard about her disappearance? Would she turn her away?

The watchman was returning with a little, wiry woman, whose crinkled face gazed keenly at her. She was dressed poorly, more so than her niece who, despite her long journey, was wearing a good dress and a warm shawl that Sidara had given her as a parting present. But Esther saw kindness at the back of her gaze and her heart beat fast in hope.

"So you are my sister's child?" the woman said and, coming up to her, she gazed into her face and then started. "Why," she cried, "It is Esther!"

"Yes, Aunt."

"But you are drowned!" exclaimed the woman. "The story reached here a long time ago that you were drowned on your wedding morning."

It was the first time Esther's thoughts had been deliberately recalled to that time, the first time she had heard what had been thought in her home circles as to her disappearance, and she retreated a step, confused and uncertain what to say. Her aunt grasped her arms and looked searchingly at her.

"You are indeed Esther," she said. "Tell my why such a story was believed."

Esther, in her turn, looked down into the eyes of her aunt and saw only goodwill and kindness so she answered unsteadily.

"I ran away. I did not know that the story had been told."

"And your husband?"

"He was drowned," Esther said with an effort. She could not continue, but something in her face restrained Hanna from asking any further question.

"Peace, child. You shall not speak of it now," she said and taking her into her arms, she kissed her. "Are you not as

one risen from the dead? Come into the kitchens and meet
my companions."

"But you are working?"

"No matter. Is it every day I have my sister's child restored
to me?" She took her arm and led her into the kitchens
where several were working.

"See what has come to me!" she cried. "My sister's child!"
They were kind and came to greet her. They exclaimed
over her slenderness and her beauty, but suddenly a tall,
big woman came in angrily.

"What is this?" she demanded. "Is the Mistress to wait for
her food? The hour is past." The workers scattered to their
tasks, but Hanna said,

"My sister's child has come, Mistress Fonteye."

"May God give you health," the woman said, looking
Esther up and down briefly, then to Hanna, "Let your joy
be later. The child may sit in your house until the hour of
food is past."

As she went out, Hanna smiled at Esther. "The watchman
will take you to my house," she said. "Wait there. I shall
not be long."

Led to one of the small houses that were set back against
the compound wall, Esther entered it thankfully and sat
down. Left alone, she got her book out and fingered it.
More than ever these days it was becoming her talisman
and comfort. Hesitantly, for it was still a new idea to her,
she offered thanks to her new-found Saviour for leading her
safely there.

When her aunt came, Esther got up. Hanna smiled at her.
"Blow up the fire, child, and we will eat," she said. "Have
you come from your parents' house?"

Esther knelt to make up the fire. "No," she answered. "I
have not been home since—since that day."

"What?" cried her aunt. "Have you not even sent word?
Do they still think you dead?"

"If that is what they think, yes," she answered quietly.

"So where have you been? What have you done?"

"I have been in the lowlands," Esther answered. A little bright flame sprang up under her fingers and lit up her face. Her aunt stared at her.

"Who have you lived with?" she asked. "Had your father relations there?"

"No," Esther said and did not look up. There was a pause. "Why have you left?" the woman then said and her tone was colder. "Are you expecting a child?"

"No," Esther said again as calmly as she could, and rose to her feet. "What shall I put on the fire?" Her aunt indicated a pan of split peas and Esther, adding water from a jar nearby, put it over the now-burning fire. Then she turned to her aunt.

"You have a right to know the truth," she said quietly. "I have been living the life of a woman of the streets for some years past. I ran away from my husband on the night of my wedding, as we began the descent to the lowlands. In following me, he fell into a pool and I could not pull him out to safety." She paused.

"And then?" Hanna asked. "You were afraid to return home, I think. Where did you go?"

"Some traders took me to a place called Mulata. I became a servant to—to a woman. For two years and more I served her: then, one night, she—sold me, and I started to work as she did."

"Did you bear a child?"

"No."

"Why have you left this place now?"

Esther paused to consider her answer.

"I met one who taught from the Word of God," she said finally. "He said that God had a plan for every child of His, and that we had to find it and follow it. He said it was never the way of sin."

Her aunt was silent. This was something new to her.

"The woman I worked for was to bear a child in the father's

house," went on Esther. "I remembered that my mother had once whispered to me that you lived here and I might seek you if I was destitute. So I left this place and came here."

This last, Hanna understood and she smiled at the girl.

"I would never turn from my door my own flesh and blood," she said. "But I may not gain permission for you to stay here unless you have work about the compound."

"And is it possible to find such work? I care not what I do, so that it is not what I have been doing."

Hanna hesitated long and then said slowly:

"The Lady Elizabeth needs a servant girl. We have been asked to look for a young girl willing for this work."

"It is God's provision!" Esther exclaimed in delight, but something in her aunt's face stopped her. "What is the matter?" she asked. "Is there something else?"

"No, the work is as I have told you," Hanna said, "but you should know that the Lady Elizabeth is neither a just nor a kind mistress. Your pay will be little, your hours long, and you will be as the dirt beneath her feet."

"I care not for that," Esther said impetuously. "Can anything be worse than the work from which I have come?"

"I cannot answer that," her aunt said, "but I know the child who has left ran away because she could not bear it longer. We in the kitchen see little of the Mistress, but those near her have suffered much under the steward, Job, who acts for her."

"The steward?"

"There are two head servants," explained Hanna. "The housekeeper, Fonteye, you have met: she appears hard, but has a kind heart. The steward, Job, is a cruel man."

Esther stood silent, knowing suddenly what lay behind her aunt's words. Hanna looked at her. "You understand, I see," she said. "The last servant-girl he took to himself. When she wept, he beat her and she fled."

"God can protect me," Esther said slowly. "But if—if I

should again be taken at a man's will, I think I would die."
There was a moment's silence. Then she spoke again.
"Speak for me," she said. "I will try."

Later that afternoon, Esther was called into the presence of
the housekeeper. Hanna took her to the room and left her
there. The girl bowed, and was silent.

"Well, lift your head up, child! Let me see you!" was the
first thing Fonteye said, in an intimidating tone and, as
Esther obediently raised her head, she added, "Well, you
look well enough. The Mistress likes a good-looking face
about her."

Esther's expression did not change. Had she not often
been argued about in Sidara's house while she had stood
there, mute and uncaring.

"What service have you had?"

"I have served since I was a child, mistress," answered
Esther calmly.

"Where and with whom? Did your parents put you into such
service?"

"In a town named Mulata: a woman named Sidara,"
Esther said. "I was her only servant and learned to cook
and to serve and to care for her clothes."

"And your parents?"

"My parents live in the highlands of Zoah," Esther replied.
"They married me to a man of the lowlands who died shortly
after I had wed him. That is why I entered service."

"Or did you run away from your husband?"

"I have told you the truth," Esther answered. She looked
fully at the woman as she spoke. And she did not like such a
look and said angrily:

"You will have to learn not to stand in such a proud posture
before the Mistress, or she will not keep you a day. Such
bold looks may have done very well in your previous work,
but they will not be endured here."

Esther felt the blood rise to her cheeks, but she nevertheless
bent her head.

D

"I would study to be what my mistress desired," she said. "I have been nothing else but a servant since I left my home."

There was a pause, while the woman appeared to consider. Then she said, "You may come to the house at six o'clock this evening. It will be the Mistress's decision as to whether she will employ you."

The woman referred to as the Lady Elizabeth was the wife of a Provincial Governor who spent most of his time in the city, paying only the briefest of visits to his home. She was middle-aged, fat and supremely selfish. Exceedingly conscious of her own dignity and position, she condescended to notice those who were in her employ only when, for some reason, they were not where she expected them to be. In that case, if they were children, she ordered Job to beat them; if they were not children, then their already-meagre wages were cut with a total disregard for the effect of such a cut on their dependants. Because work was scarce, she did not lack servants.

But all this, Esther had yet to learn. Admitted to her presence, Esther bowed deeply and stood in silence for the Mistress to speak.

"What is your name, child?"

"Esther, lady."

"You are the niece of one of the cooks?"

"Yes, lady."

"Are you accustomed to house service?"

"Yes, lady."

"And you will work hard and well?"

"I will try, lady."

"Then let it be." The woman waved a fat, bejewelled hand. The housekeeper pushed Esther forward with a gesture and the girl, realising what was expected of her, knelt to kiss the Mistress's podgy feet in their thick, black shoes.

"Come at five tomorrow," was all the housekeeper said to her when they had left the room.

So began a new kind of life for Esther. It was fortunate she
had long been accustomed to hard work, for her day now
began at five, when she kindled the charcoal burner for her
mistress's room and often did not end until after nine at
night. She found it difficult to find time even to eat her
midday meal. And yet she was not always busy. She would
spend hours standing against the wall by the door of the
Mistress's room, simply in case the Lady Elizabeth desired a
cup of wine or another rug beneath her feet.

She was a personal servant. She would dress the Mistress in
the morning, braid and oil her hair. She would bring water
for her to wash her hands and face and then kneel to wash
her feet for her. She stood behind her chair at meal-times,
and ran back and forward to the kitchen throughout the
day for food and drink of one sort or another. She kept the
flies off her mistress if she chose to sit outside; she would
carry her possessions behind her if she went from one room
to another; she polished certain ornaments that the Mistress
wished other servants not to touch. Most irritating of all,
she was never off duty. Even when the Mistress slept after
lunch, Esther had to stand by the door in case she should
wake up and desire something. She had not been there for a
week before she encountered the steward.

She had seen him, of course, for she had often been present
when he had discussed business affairs with the Mistress.
She had felt his hot gaze upon her once or twice, but had
kept her own gaze lowered, offering a frightened prayer in
her heart. He had made no attempt to speak with her until
one day when she received a summons to his presence.

It was about two o'clock on a hot afternoon and the Mistress
was asleep, when one of the compound watchmen came with
a message to Esther that she was wanted in the steward's
office. The watchman was an undersized, rather timid
man and he muttered the message with averted eyes.

"I cannot leave my mistress without her permission,"
Esther answered him quietly.

"It would be foolish in you to disobey Job," the man told her. "You may tell the Mistress that he summoned you, can you not?" and he left.

For a moment Esther hesitated. The Mistress was sound asleep and not likely to wake. The kitchens were near at hand. She would ask her aunt.

Hanna was busy washing up, but listened to her and said at once,

"You will have to go. He will be a bad enemy to make, and it is probably only to sign your contract. Have you done that since you came here?"

"No," Esther said doubtfully. "Very well. I will go."

Job was alone when she came, and, when she entered and bowed, he rose to his feet. She saw a greasy book open in front of him and thought her aunt must have been right. There was a pause that lengthened until Esther felt she must break it.

"You called me, sir," she said.

"It is necessary to write in this book that you have entered employment here," he said. "What is your name?"

"Esther Felagi, sir," she answered and he wrote it down, bending over the table.

"You must not call me 'sir': my name is Job," he said then, smiling at her. "I hope we will be friends." His eyes ran up and down her body in unmistakable appreciation, and he laughed as the anger leapt to her eyes.

"Come, let us not misunderstand one another," he said straightly. "It is well known from what work you have come here. It will not be hard to share our pleasures." He took a step towards her but she recoiled and retreated to the doorway.

"It is true that I once did not care who lay at my side," she said, direct in her turn. "But I have left that work and my body is not at any man's call now. If you have no more business with me, I must return to my mistress."

He smiled, seeming to like this speech.

"Come, we shall do well for each other," he said. "I like a little spirit. But you must not oppose me, you know, child. I can make life very difficult for you if I choose."

"Then do so," Esther said. "I have a God who can keep me pure and He is ten thousand times as powerful as you." She did not wait to see his reaction to this, but hurried back to the big house. Her foot was on the step when she heard the Mistress's voice:

"Esther! Esther! Where is that lazy girl?"

Her heart beating hard, Esther entered the room. The Lady Elizabeth was on her feet, angry and shouting.

"Where have you been?" she demanded when the girl came in. "What right have you to leave the room without my permission? What do I pay you wages for—to follow your own pleasures when I need you to wait on me?"

These shouts brought Fonteye into the room. Used to her mistress's rages, she coaxed her to sit down again. She did so, but still talked indignantly.

"Am I to be left alone as soon as I rest? What if I need something? Do I have to shout for my needs?"

Esther was standing helplessly in the middle of the room. When the Mistress had calmed down a little, Fonteye turned to her.

"What have you to say?" she asked curtly.

"The steward commanded my attendance, lady," Esther said nervously. "I did not know whether I should go, but decided in the end that I should enquire what it was he wanted. Forgive me. I have not knowingly done wrong."

Fonteye nodded and looked back at the Mistress as if expecting her to accept this.

"The girl is new, lady," she was beginning, when she was interrupted.

"Lies! It is all lies!" said a mocking voice and Job walked into the room, smiling sardonically. The Mistress looked at him and Esther started. Her heart beat hard.

"What do you mean, Job?" the Mistress demanded, suddenly alert. "Did you not send for this girl?"

"I have never sent for her," he said coolly, looking Esther full in the face.

"He did send for me," Esther said breathlessly. "The watchman gave me the message. I have just come back from his room."

Job's expression did not change.

"Which watchman?" he said contemptuously.

"The old man," she answered, and to the Mistress, "Call him, my lady. He will tell you that I have told the truth."

"There is no need," said the Mistress stiffly but Job had already sent a shout ringing for the watchman. He entered, servile, afraid.

"Now, man, tell the Mistress that this slut is lying when she says I sent for her this afternoon," Job said lazily. Esther stared at him. He was so confident that he did not even put a threat into his tone of voice. The man glanced nervously at him and did not look at Esther.

"Come, fellow," the Lady Elizabeth said, "Did you call this girl from her post?"

"No," he said. "I took no message."

Esther felt dizzy.

"But you did," she began when Job dropped his lazy pose and turned fiercely on her.

"Silence, jade!" he said. "Is not one lie enough for you? You dare to use my name to cover your own disobedience and laziness? You shall feel the rod on your back to teach you who is your master."

"No, no. She is no child," interposed Fonteye unexpectedly. "Cut her wages if you will, but do not beat her. It is not fitting for a girl of her years." They looked upon Esther standing flushed and angry.

"She will be better tamed by the rod," Job said. "Liars must be taught to curb their tongues."

He had perhaps intended to goad Esther further and he

succeeded. She had seen falsehood and deceit in plenty
before, but none so blatant as this.

"You dare call me liar!" she exclaimed, forgetting caution
in her blazing indignation. "You, who lie only out of spite
because I would not give myself to you."

He hit her with the back of his hand and she staggered
back against the wall.

"Enough! Enough!" the Lady Elizabeth said sharply.
"Mistress Fonteye, you shall chastise the girl. See that she
returns to me immediately afterwards." She bent her cold
gaze on Esther. "You must learn to be obedient," she said,
"and to curb that angry tongue." In the housekeeper's
room, Esther spoke.

"Mistress Fonteye, do you believe me?"

"If I did, it would avail you little," Fonteye replied. "My
only care is to obey the Mistress."

"And beat me for something I have not done?"

The older woman looked down at her with a certain compassion, but her voice did not soften.

"You have chosen to work here," she said. "These are the
conditions under which you will work. If you wish to
escape punishment, you may go to your aunt's house,
collect your things, and leave within the hour. It is in your
hands."

"My hands?" thought Esther, "or God's hands? Did he
not lead me here?"

Returning to the Mistress, when it was over, she knelt at her
feet as she had been told to do, but the words she must use
to sue for forgiveness choked in her throat, and she felt a
rage in her heart which surprised her. Was this, in truth,
the best life held for her? Was she to turn from prostitution
only to slavery? Her thoughts turned, as they often did these
days, to her new-found Saviour. "Lord Jesus," she said
within herself, "can it be that you are with me even *here*?"
She knew the answer immediately for such a warmth, such
a peace filled her heart that as she at last rose from her

knees, even the Mistress frowning at her, wondered at the serenity and joy on her face.

But the battle was not over. Often her aunt, coming into the house at night, saw in the light of the oil lamp tear stains on the girl's face and once her lips were so bruised that she could not speak without pain.

"Esther, let me send word to your parents," she pleaded. "They will receive you again. Why should you suffer here?"

"I will never go home," was her only answer.

"But why—when your life is so hard here?"

Why stay? Esther pondered often over the sense of compulsion that she felt to stay in Engadi. Would not a return to her former life be preferable to her present service? She only knew in her heart that God had led her there when she had given her life to Him, and that it could not be right to run away from the first test He had laid on her. She was wary of Job now, knowing that he only sought opportunity to set her wrong with the Mistress. She was outwardly quiet and obedient, but often within was a raging storm of resentment and fury at the petty tyranny of the Mistress, and the hardness of her tasks.

★

ESTHER had never heard the words of the Saviour, "Follow me," but she followed as I had done, because the fear of stepping off the path of His will into those misty, leaderless regions of self-will, was greater than the fear of following her Master even into the mouth of hell itself.

6 · The Gates of Jerusalem

WHAT IS IT *that eludes me?*
What is it that I seek?
Why does this ceaseless throbbing rage my brain?
Why does my soul reach longingly
Through prison bars of Pain?

"MISSIONARIES!" I moved restlessly on my chair and studied my new colleagues. It was an inter-mission prayer meeting and I had been in the country for just five days. "Ugh!" I thought. "Will I get to look like that? Will I learn to wear that expression of amiability? Will my shoes get to be that flat-heeled? Will I ever wear white ankle-socks and scrape my hair back like that?"

We got up for tea. I stood awkwardly holding a cup in one hand and shaking hands with the other as I was introduced to one and another. A little woman, hearing that I had only just come, said in a voice just dripping with enthusiasm, "Oh my *dear!* Aren't you just *thrilled* to be here?" I was so amazed, I nearly let fall my cup.

"Er—no," I said. "No, I don't think so."

For six weeks I stayed in the mission headquarters. As is every recruit to some degree, I was bewildered, nervous, and homesick, although trying to put on as calm a front as possible. One Sunday I went to an American service and we sang a hymn which I have never forgotten.

O Thou, in whose presence my soul takes delight,
On whom, in affliction, I call,

My comfort by day and my song in the night,
My hope, my salvation, my all!

Where dost thou, dear Shepherd, resort with thy sheep,
To feed them in pastures of love?
Say, why in the valley of death should I weep,
Or alone in this wilderness rove?

Why should I wander an alien from thee,
Or cry in the desert for bread?
Thy foes will rejoice when my sorrows they see,
And smile at the tears I have shed.

Dear Shepherd! I hear, and will follow thy call;
I know the sweet sound of thy voice;
Restore and defend me, for thou art my all,
And in thee, I will ever rejoice.

Others were listening to the sermon when I was memorising that hymn! Why should I behave as if I were alone in this wilderness? Why should I cry in this 'desert' for something to satisfy my heart-ache? Are not the minions of Satan rejoicing to see my tears? I lifted my head again. I *knew* the 'sweet sound of His voice' and He could both restore and defend me in this new place, among these strangers. When I went to my first station, it was with a greater determination than ever to take hold of 'His strength', for I knew He could carry me through.

I once spent a glorious white night on a balcony in Jordan. We had travelled all day down the coast road in the hot sun, we had climbed slowly up through the valleys of erstwhile Judea, we had stood for an hour or more in the dusty and windy no-man's land of the Mandlebaum Gate, looking at the sandbags and bullet-marked houses of the deserted compound, and now at last we had reached a hotel in Jordan. I was tired, but I could not sleep. We were outside the old city of Jerusalem but from the balcony of my room I could look across at Herod's gate, one of the entrances

into the old city. How many years had I desired to enter the
city of God! How long had it been the goal of my desires
and dreams! Jerusalem: along whose streets had walked
kings, prophets, emperors. Jerusalem: to whom the eyes of
the faithful had looked for over a thousand years. Jerusalem:
witness of my Lord's death and most glorious resurrection.
And I was within a few hours of entering!

Since then, I have often thought of that occasion as a
parable. That night spent on the balcony in Jordan is the
first few years of a missionary's life when, usually, little real
work can be done and the recruit looks at the future work.
He has glimpses of what the future can hold, but he does
not do more than approach these joys. It is in these years
that the recruit makes the involuntary decision as to
whether, when they are over, the gates of Jerusalem will
swing open, or whether they will spend all their missionary
lives outside the walls of the desired and beloved city where
they would be. Whether, to be plainer, their missionary
service is going to be joyful, successful, empowered by the
Holy Spirit, or whether they are going to be one of that
tribe of ineffective but vaguely well-meaning missionaries
who are rarely troubled with real attacks of Satan because it
is hardly worth his while to bother with them. Whether we
are going to 'walk in the Spirit' or to cling to the things of
the flesh.

One sentence I read in that missionary classic *Ambassadors
for Christ* I committed to memory. "If a missionary recruit
can, in the early days, be deflected one hair's breadth from
the straight course, later years will bring him wide of the
mark and he can be left to pursue his devious course un-
molested." Let every missionary ask himself or herself, "Am
I being deflected? Have I started on that path which leads
away from the highest? Is my primary aim to lead men and
women to trust in the Saviour and am I doing all I can to
bring it about? Or have I another aim: to build a fine
school, to see a clinic, a hospital, established, to organise a

printing press?" These things are all very well, as long as they remain a means to an end . . . the end that the people to whom we have been sent may find Christ.

"One hair's breadth!" Let us glance at the pressures that build up around a missionary recruit. I have written elsewhere about some of the more obvious difficulties a recruit has to face and I will not refer to them again, but just share some of the insidious 'thought-traps' that lie in wait for the unwary recruit. By 'thought-traps' I mean when your thoughts take a certain direction to the extent of trapping you into making a wrong decision, and lead you to dissatisfaction with the will of God.

There is the 'am-I-wasting-my-life?' thought-trap. This is particularly tempting when the recruit in question has had a reasonably good training and education for work in the home country; and furthermore, has well-meaning but mistaken friends who write suggesting that to be stuck out in the middle of nowhere among savages, is a criminal waste of money spent on your Western education. Certainly, in the place I was first sent to on the mission field, it would be hard indeed not to wonder sometimes whether one was mistaken about the Lord's call. To compare that place with the busy, teeming, Western world that I had left would be like comparing a small, shallow, stagnant little back-water of the Thames with the open sea.

The houses were built of mud, the roofs of grass or (if you were wealthier) of tin. There were no proper roads, no electric light, no piped water, no attempt at a sanitation scheme: and this in a town of 10,000 or more people. What place has the product of the Western world here, unless it be to do something practical about raising the standard of living? What place has an impractical graduate, a teacher, a writer? Hardly any of the people around can read and many cannot even speak the language you are sweating to learn.

Basically, I knew better, of course. I was often happy in

those days in the fellowship of the Bible school students, but then I would be jolted and horrified to get a letter demanding what I was doing in a back-water of Africa, 'teaching illiterate niggers to read'. There was a constant tug-of-war in my heart. I remember reading something I took note of in the life of a man called Ragland:

"What if we waste our lives? Down the steep mountain sides, scores of waterfalls race in joyful, eager streams. From our valley halfway up the heights we can see them spring from their secret places among the crags a thousand feet above. We can watch them in their headlong flight to the river here. Shall the waterfalls do more for their river than we are willing to do for our Lord? The joy of life, the strength of youth, the gathered fruit of study, the powers of the whole being and all its riches of love: are these too much to pour forth upon him at the feet of our Lord, our Redeemer?"

Another thought-trap centres around the question of restriction. It was just not easy for a foreign woman to go wandering around the country-side alone. It would not be understood. My work did not at that early stage take me out, so I was to all intents and purposes confined within the compound. Sometimes it was indeed as if prison walls had closed in on me. Accustomed, in England, to changing my surroundings as often as I chose, suddenly I realised that I could not go out unless I found a companion. This was, at first, frustrating and difficult. Recently I found, scribbled on the back of one of my early language notebooks, the words of Lovelace:

"*Stone walls do not a prison make,*
Nor iron bars a cage.
Minds, innocent and quiet, take
That for a hermitage."

I have never been in a prison. Perhaps if I had, I would laugh at the comparison of a home and garden with a real prison, and rightly so. Yet even so, the above words are applicable. But you need this 'hermitage' in one way. You need this time of slow adjustment. I have sometimes thought how merciful it is that a new missionary is hampered in his speech because of a lack of language. What blunders we would make, what offence we could give, if from the moment we came, people could understand us and our opinions. We must be patient and wait: watch, learn, prepare, and then, in His time, not ours, fit into the gap in the team of missionaries that is widening for our entry.

Other things, too, go under the heading of restrictions: restriction of diet, of dress, of (obviously) speech. To a large extent, freedom of decision is no longer yours, for you couldn't carry out your own ideas anyway. There is restriction of employment (and it is only one coming from a background where it was Bridge or nothing, who could fully appreciate the horrors of Scrabble). There is restriction of companions too. My 'cell-mates' treated me with kindly forbearance, but I found myself quickly irritated with them, quick to criticise, impatient that they did not share my own enthusiasms over certain things. Once a contemporary of mine from another mission paid me a short visit and we played 'pop' records in a little hut, separated from my older colleagues, and talked into the night. My impatience over the situation I was in was very near flame those days, and it is entirely due to the patience of my colleagues, that on the whole it was kept smouldering.

It was not all like this, however. Sometimes I loved it. Sometimes I remembered that souls were precious to my Master and rejoiced that I was surrounded by such needy ones. Sometimes I remembered to look ahead to a time when I would see that the hand of God had guided me through these early trials to a real work for Him in this land. But more often, I did not. Things were not well. How could they be, when there was smouldering beneath an oft-changing front a feeling of anger that the Lord had forced me to come out here in the first place. Behaviour which was flagrantly childish one moment and bitterly repentant the next, was not conducive to spiritual growth. And then it was as if the Lord said, "Very well. You are not learning the lessons that I wanted you to. You are always, at the back of your mind, wishing you were at home. Very well. Go home. Take another look at your Egypt: at the fish, the cucumbers, the melons, and decide finally if that is what you want."

In the same month in which I had first received the call of God, eighteen months after I had first come to the field, a letter from my father said my mother was in bed with a slight temperature. Five days later, he wrote that she had gone to hospital with what was thought to be a minor infection. A few days later I heard that she had incurable cancer and, almost with that letter, came a telegram summoning me home. She was going to die.

Whether she knew whether I had come or not no one could be certain for she was past speech when I reached her side. I spent four days by her bed, reading and praying with her before the Lord took her. Afterwards all my thoughts had to be for my father who was numbed by the suddenness of the tragedy. I realised I could not soon return overseas, and that I had to look for work in England. It was as if the Lord said: "Look well at this place and choose then whether it shall be my will for you, or whether you will live in this land and enjoy what it offers." So I looked.

*

ONE DAY, Hanna, returning from one of her mornings at the market, greeted Esther with excitement.

"Esther! Guess who I met in town today: Joseph Geneta!" She went on to tell her something else, but Esther did not hear. Joseph! How many years had passed since she had let

herself think of him? Her former playmate; comforter of
her childish griefs; teller of stories about the One she had,
even in those early days, learned to love. He was a reminder
of those happier days when she was unburdened with anything worse than her mother's quick temper; and the
remembrance of them swept over her like a flood.

"What is he doing here?" she asked at last.

"Haven't you been listening?" cried her aunt in despair.
"Here I have told you everything and not one word have
you heard!"

"I'm sorry. Tell me again."

Her aunt glared at her in exasperation and then began to
tell her. Joseph was working for some foreigners, who em-
ployed him to sell books. He and a friend had come to
Engadi because the yearly festival of the great church in the
holy place was due on Monday. As all other traders did,
Joseph would be selling his wares then and talking with the
people who would be gathering from all over the country to
attend the festival.

"He did not know me at first," went on her aunt, "but he
was talking with a great crowd of people and I stopped to
listen and look at the pictures he was holding up. Then
someone in the crowd called out to know where he was
from and when he said 'Zoah', I knew who he was, for you
know I was with your mother and father for that long time
many years ago and I knew his father."

She paused expectantly and seemed waiting for a question,
but Esther, her head bowed, her thoughts confused and
troubled, did not ask it.

"Esther, what is it?" her aunt said, puzzled. "Are you such
an unnatural child that you do not care to hear news of
your parents after these many years. Will you not ask?"

"Yes, I will ask," Esther said then, looking steadily at her.
"What news has he brought?"

"They are well and have moved to a house in Bali. Your
father now has found employment with the same foreigners

that Joseph is working for. Tara—"

'Tara!' thought Esther. 'Dear little Tara!'

"has started school in Bali."

Esther smiled rather twistedly. So Tara had achieved what she had begged for unavailingly, what she still desired above all.

"I told Joseph you were here," went on Hanna. "He was at first difficult to convince, for he believed with everyone that you were drowned. But now he is impatient to see you."

"How is that possible?" Esther said half-bitterly.

"I said you were working here and found it difficult to get any time off," nodded Hanna, "but that you would be at the festival on Monday."

"Will I?" Esther said, surprised.

"Of course you will, you silly child," Hanna said. "Everyone goes. It is the biggest event of the year. The Master will come tomorrow and many of his friends. For us, it is a very busy time. The Lady Elizabeth goes and all of her servants with her."

The next day the Master came, driven in style, with three other cars full of friends and relations. The house, big though it was, was filled. Even with extra help from outside, the servants were run off their feet. Esther saw the Master for the first time at the midday meal: a short, podgy man, with greying hair and a kind manner. He did not notice her, even when she held the water for him to rinse his hands, but talked in a slow, rumbling voice to those who had come with him, and to his wife, who greeted him with dignified affection.

On Monday, the day of the festival, Fonteye told her to dress in her best and prepare to accompany the Mistress.

"But what shall I do?" Esther asked.

"Nothing!" snorted the housekeeper. "We all do nothing! We walk behind my lady and stop when she stops, and carry a spare pair of shoes and an umbrella in case it rains."

This forecast turned out to be true and Esther, walking

slowly in this group with others whom she had never seen but who were evidently distant relations and their servants, despaired in the crush of ever setting eyes on Joseph. They arrived at the church and Esther gazed with awe at the white building with its gold dome gleaming in the sun. The husband and wife separated there with the affable dignity which seemed to characterise their every movement. The Mistress was waved into the church and Esther wondered whether they were to follow.

"No. We wait here!" hissed one of the others.

The service began and Esther looked desperately around for Joseph, but the men's section of the church compound was largely out of sight of the women's and she could not see him. She saw her aunt, however, and edged over to be near her.

"Will I get any time free?" she whispered.

Hanna smiled understandingly. "When the Mistress goes for her midday meal at the big house," she whispered back. "The servants there will not need your help. Unless the Mistress herself commands you, you can wait outside and the feast goes on for many hours."

This was found to be true and at the hour following the noon meal, with the sun still high in the sky, Esther slipped away and began her search. And thus she came upon Joseph who was wandering down a lane which led from the healing waters.

"Joseph!" she exclaimed, and stared at him. Where she had left a tousled youth chopping wood for his mother, she found a tall, self-possessed young man, dressed in white clothes as befitted the feast day and looking at her with the same kind of wonder as she looked at him.

"Esther!" He bent and kissed her, holding her arms in a vice-like grip, the only thing which showed the intensity of his emotion.

"How you have changed!" she gasped, and grasped his hands.

"But you," Joseph answered, "you have risen from the dead! You are well?"

"Well enough," answered Esther, and her glance wavered from his. "Tell me what has happened to you and your parents?"

"My father and mother are well. Two of my brothers have gone to the city to school and I have been in this work for three years. But you? What happened on that day you left? Come and let us sit and talk a while."

They walked a little way off the path and sat under a tree. Here, for the first time, Esther told the full story of the past five years to this, her childhood companion. He listened without comment. Only when she told him of the preacher and the help he had given her which had made her determine to leave Sidara, did he look up with a smile of real happiness. When she had finished, she would not look at him.

"I have not prayed for you," Joseph said gently after a while, "for I have thought you dead. But God has cared for you just the same and brought you out of the pit to set your feet upon the rock."

Esther looked at him, puzzled.

"It is what the Bible says," he explained.

"Oh, you can read! You can read my book to me!" she cried. "It is the book which your father gave me. I still have it."

"It is that book, among others, that I sell," Joseph said, and opened the satchel he was carrying to show her. "This is the Bible," he said, "and these are little parts of the Bible."

She fingered them, awestruck. She had not seen so many books together before. "Oh, how learned you must be. How wonderful it would be to read these. Read to me . . . oh!" she suddenly remembered the passing time. "I cannot stay, Joseph, my mistress—"

"Yes," he said. "Your aunt told me you were in service: but Esther, have you not considered that it is time you went home?"

There was a long pause.

"I will never do that," she said, and a hardness had stiffened her very body as she spoke. "They cast me out as you might an unwanted dog or cat. They cared nothing for my agony and pain. I shall never go back."

Joseph looked at her with a kind of pity. "Esther," he said. "Did you not tell me just now of that wonderful day when you heard your sins could be forgiven because Jesus had died for you?"

"Yes," she said wonderingly.

"Then let me read you some more of that book you so desire to read," he said and he opened it and read: "Forgive us our sins in the same measure that we forgive others their sins." For a moment he paused. Then he added, "It means that only if we are ready to forgive those we think have wronged us, will the Lord forgive us for what we have done against Him. Your parents are believers now: you would find they would welcome you."

She would not meet his eyes.

"Esther, do not harbour hatred in your heart," he pleaded. "It destroys not the hated but the hater."

Still she said nothing.

He waited and then sighed. "I shall go home tomorrow," he said. "And I shall tell your parents that you are with your aunt and working in a big household. What you tell them after that is your own affair. Don't you want to go home? Do you want to go on working here? What do you want?"

"I want to learn to read!" Esther burst out, her longing written on every line of her face. "I want to understand the One whom I follow. I want to serve Him and tell others about the way He has helped me. That is what I want!"

He stared at her, surprised at her outburst. Then he said slowly. "There is a school in Bali for girls such as you, run by the people for whom I work."

Esther stared, and looked at him with a sudden excitement.

"Is that where Tara goes?" she asked.

"No. She goes to the Government school. This is a Bible School where the Bible is taught."

"I would learn to read it?"

"Certainly."

"Could I go to it?"

"I don't see why not. You would have to pay fees, of course, but they are not high."

"If I prayed, God would show me how to pay the fees," she said with simple faith.

Joseph smiled. "But then you would have to come home," he reminded her.

She was silent.

"Don't you think God might also show you how to do that?" suggested Joseph.

She gave a reluctant smile but did not answer. A number of people passed down the path and it made her remember her position.

"I must go now," she said, and rose.

Joseph rose with her. "Come, I will take you back," he said. She walked behind him down the narrow path, her thoughts leaping ahead to a future suddenly brightening, as the dark clouds of the night lighten to the rays of the dawn.

7 · This is the Way: Walk ye in it

It may be Thou wilt grant me times of peace,
With joys untold my pathway daily fill;
And I will laugh with gladdened heart, and sing,
BUT IF NOT *I will love Thee still.*

It may be I shall feel Thine arms beneath,
In times of loneliness when joy seems past;
And I will know myself raised up.
BUT IF NOT *I will hold Thee fast.*

It may be I shall see Thy plan unfold,
And know the path on which my feet are set,
And go forth confident with loving hope,
BUT IF NOT *I will trust Thee yet.*

BUT IF *Thou dost allow the furnace fire*
To burn away all dross as of small worth,
How precious are Thy waiting, healing hands,
How wonder-full our suffering on earth.

I WAS HOME: IN ENGLAND. If I did not choose to, I need never return to the mission field. This was, after all, one of the *bona fide* reasons for being a returned missionary (I shied away from the term 'missionary casualty' that I had heard in Wycliffe). There would not be the nasty murmuring that attended other people's return: ". . . not up to it, you know . . . a mental strain . . . my dear, she was just *impossible* to live with. . . ."

My father was on the verge of retiring. My only brother had a young family and, although he lived nearby at present, he would be moving away the following year. I was the only daughter, unmarried, and very close to my father. The situation was immediately clear to a number of my friends. I should give up any thought of the mission field and make a home for my father.

But where was the joy that should have attended such a general opinion? I was out of my prison. I was back among my chosen friends. Bookshops, art-galleries abounded. I was no longer stared at everywhere I went. My speech was immediately understood. I was among the cultural pattern in which I had been brought up. Where then was the joy that should have attended all this? Where was the feeling of relief that I had escaped so honourably the horrors of the mission field?

I took a job teaching senior English in a girls' private school in the country near my home. It was an environment I was thoroughly at home in: not surprisingly, since it was the same school that I had attended for ten years as a pupil. Although at first I was somewhat wary of a girls' school, the staff-room, largely composed of married women, was one of the sanest I have ever been in and free of the pettiness which can make such a place intolerable. I was teaching the kind of girl I liked and understood. I was being paid four times as much as I received abroad. I was using this precious Western education that people were always writing about when I was abroad. Why then, when I looked at sixth-formers strolling about the grounds in their school blazers, discussing the latest record or boy-friend, did I see thin, poorly-clad girls, already women, waiting their turn to fill their heavy water pots at the thin trickle of water that was the spring? Why, when I was marking the attempts of the fifth form at rendering 'To be or not to be' into modern English, did the verbs of another language form themselves on the paper? Why, when I

looked over a class of pleasant-faced and likeable girls, did
I see the dull apathetic faces of country-women, 'having no
hope and without God'? As the doors of the mission field
began to swing shut upon me, so I sprang at them and tried
with all my strength to keep them open. Humbly, fearfully,
I approached the Lord. "Send me back . . . trust me again
. . . I will do better. . . ."

Slowly at first, then with increasing confidence, I began to
make arrangements to go back. I fixed on a date in the
autumn which meant I would have stayed at home for
eighteen months. I met opposition from some, who did not
scruple to tell me openly that they considered my duty lay
at home; others quietly encouraged me and steadily prayed
me on. Within, was a growing confidence that my decision
to return was right. My father, though knowing fully what
it would mean for him, was steadfast in his opinion that I
must do what I felt to be right. Nothing to him would have
been worse than for me to 'sacrifice my career' for him.
But although he said "Just leave me, I'll manage", I felt
I could not do that. He was not domesticated in any
way and I could not contemplate leaving him to live alone.
He did not want to leave the house he had lived in with my
mother, but it was far too big for one man. Tenants seemed
the answer. They were not difficult to find, but all sorts of
horrid possibilities came to mind. A young couple, who
would be tolerant of, but wholly unconcerned about, their
landlord; older people, already set in their ways, who could
make life really unhappy for a single person; and so on. Time
grew desperately short. I would not go without a workable
arrangement being made: it seemed impossible that it could
be made in such a short time. But every verse I seemed to
read in the Bible those days seemed to confirm me in the
fact that I would go, that things would be arranged in time.
Ten days before I was due to leave, tenants were found:
five days before I left, they were installed. On the day I had
planned to leave, all those months before, I left. When I

exclaimed "It is the Lord's doing and it is marvellous in my eyes!" it seemed that an air of faint surprise came down from heaven.

Leaving my father, even so, was still hard. Naturally: for I was leaving him in the care of comparative strangers. His sister, however, and my brother were nearby, and I comforted myself that I could always return again if real need arose. For the first months, however, the fact that I had returned was all I could think about. Once again, I arrived by plane; once again it was to a sweet, fresh dawn. But this time, as my foot touched the tarmac of the airstrip, I could have knelt to kiss the ground beneath my feet. As I walked towards the custom shed, ready to do battle with the customs' official on the subject of my brand new tape-recorder, there was a beatific smile on my face that I could not, try as I would, remove. How often we do not truly value something until we have almost lost it.

When I reached my original station, I understood for the first time the expression 'walking on air'. The very ground seemed springy to the touch, for this sunbaked earth was where I belonged, these people were the ones the Lord had chosen to be my companions; this work, whether it was to be frowning over nouns and verbs, or teaching small, smelly boys to read, was consecrated by Him for me.

But the situation in which I had left my father was still a worry nagging at the back of all my thoughts. His letters were so determinedly cheerful, and he was obviously lonely. I imagined him coming in tired from a day at the office with no one to talk to, and having to open a tin of baked beans for his supper. Then a difficulty arose with the tenants, and I began to think I must return. There followed a month of uncertainty and worry. I remember one occasion when, a letter from my father and another from a neighbour about him in my hand, I went to a little hut where I knew I could be quite alone and I poured out my soul to the Lord, saying something like:

"Lord, what is the use of your having so wonderfully brought me back here? Am I *ever* going to feel secure here and not on the point of returning? And then people are criticising me for staying out here. Lord, it's not me they're criticising, it's you, for you brought me here!"

How patient was the Lord and how loving! Quite firmly and deliberately He brought to my notice Psalm 37, verses 3, 5, and 6:

"Trust in the Lord, and do good: so you will dwell in the land and enjoy security. . . .

Commit your way to the Lord; trust in Him and He will act. He will bring forth your vindication as the light, and your right as the noonday."

For the moment, that sufficed.

Soon after that, I had another very disturbing letter from someone else. Immediately I got worked up again. I must go, at least into the capital city where I didn't have to wait so long for post, and from where I could go off quickly if the need arose. I glanced at my daily calendar: *"He that believeth shall not make haste."*

Perhaps it was a week later when the tone of my father's letters changed altogether and he wrote very happily that he was going to remarry. The sense of relief and joy with which I received this news almost made me dizzy. *"You will dwell . . . and enjoy security. . . ."*

Now my father is happily remarried and settled, and it is as if the last shadow is off my return to the mission field.

*

ESTHER HAD GONE BACK TO HER WORK after her meeting with Joseph, confused and uncertain. There seemed within her reach now an opportunity to do what she had long desired to do: to learn to read and, in particular, to read the Word of God. A picture of classrooms, teachers, books and other students would sometimes fill her mind, but then beside it would come a picture of her father's stern unyielding face as he had sent her off so many years before. "They are believers now," Joseph had said, but what did that mean? They were still the same people. "Only if you forgive others, will the Lord forgive you," said a little insistent voice inside her.

She became less attentive in her work, but the house was still so full of servants that there were plenty of others to do what she did not. Would it not be hard to leave this service, even if she decided to? Had she not some kind of contract with her employers? She had not been able to read what had been written in the big book in which she had made her mark, but she remembered the arguments that had occurred when another servant had had to leave suddenly. "Might not God also show you how to do that . .?" Joseph's face, strong, self-reliant, alight with a joy she recognised but dimly, came and went before her eyes. Tara, running to school swinging her school-bag as she had seen other children do; her mother . . .

"Esther!"

"Yes, Mistress Fonteye?"

"Call all the house servants. The Master wishes to speak with them all."

They stood in a group outside the house and the Master presently came out, with Job at his elbow.

"It has been decided," said the Master heavily, surveying them without curiosity, "that the Lady Elizabeth will accompany me to the city. From next Sunday, therefore, this house will be closed. Your Mistress, however, does not wish to dismiss her servants without notice and therefore we have decided that those who wish to do so may accompany us to the city and continue in her service. If, however, there are those among you who prefer to remain here, they are at liberty to do so and will receive a month's wages in lieu of notice."

He went within the house again, and a little buzz broke out

among the servants. Some, mostly those who had families
living in Engadi, were angry and muttered about their
contracts having been broken and taking their employers
to law. But Esther stood still, her heart leaping in her breast.
"*And you shall hear a voice behind you saying, This is the way:
walk ye in it.*"

Hanna whispered to her, "What shall we do? Do you want
to go to the city?"

And Esther turned to her, her eyes shining. "I am going
home," she said. "Come with me."

It was the time of the lesser rains and the country was
bursting into beauty. The hills were carpeted with yellow
flowers, and the big cacti plants flamed with their huge
blossoms. To Esther, the very valleys and hills seemed to be
singing with joy, and their songs were but an accompani-
ment to her own swelling heart. "Free! I am free!" she
thought and often said. Free, yes: of her years of service and
drudgery, but free too of that aching load of hatred in her
heart that she had not realised was so heavy until it had
rolled away. Hanna, half-laughing, half-gasping, would
protest:

"Esther! Slow your steps. I am an old woman. Why do you
go so fast?"

And Esther would obediently pause and let her aunt take
her young arm and reluctantly moderate her steps to those
of the older woman.

Bali was a long distance away, perhaps seven or eight
days' journey. But it was on the highland plateau and so not
an unduly dangerous journey for travellers like themselves.
Once they travelled for a day along a main road where they
got a lift from a kindly lorry-driver. They were climbing,
always climbing, until the air was clear and cool and they
were glad to wrap a blanket around themselves at night.
Then, at last, they looked far, far ahead, and saw a dark
line of trees beneath a great mountain and learned from a
passer-by that this was Bali.

"We shall not get there tonight," said Hanna firmly, for already the sun had disappeared behind the hills.

Esther agreed, and so it was in the early morning that they approached the town. Already, travellers were on the roads and dust was rising under the laden donkeys' hoofs. Suddenly Esther was struck with shyness and fear, and her steps slowed. But the Lord had prepared a fore-runner, for there, coming towards her, his familiar pack of books on his shoulder, was Joseph. He saw her and stopped so suddenly that he was surrounded by a flock of sheep coming behind him. Hanna gave a shriek of laughter as he stumbled and tripped over the indignant animals to reach them. Then he was at Esther's side.

"Welcome home, my sister in Christ," was all he said, but his eyes spoke for him. He turned to greet Hanna. Then he called the young boy who was with him, "Run ahead and tell Felagi Andinet that Esther is coming home," he bade him and the boy scampered off.

"But you were going the other way," Esther said.

"I would not go the 'other way' on a day like this," he answered, smiling at her.

The child had not only told Esther's father but it seemed all others on the way. This was not the country in which Esther had been brought up and she herself was a stranger, but it seemed her father was a man well known, for as they approached the town of Bali, many were the greetings she received and it seemed that all around her were smiling faces.

"Who are these people?" she asked Joseph.

"They are those who have been praying for you," Joseph told her and laughed at her wondering face. "You will understand one day." They entered the town.

"The Mission compound where we work is a little above the town itself," explained Joseph as they went through the market-place, being by now a group of nearly twenty. Leading from the market-place was a dusty mule-track that climbed gradually up through a wood of eucalyptus trees. As they entered this track, Esther looked up and suddenly stopped. High above, on the same road, could be seen another party of people coming towards them. She did not need Joseph's words in her ear to tell her that this was her father coming to receive her.

The two groups approached each other. Gradually, those with Esther, as if by common consent, slowed their footsteps so that Esther went before them. Hurrying down the hill, towards her, out-pacing those with him, was a tall man. Esther felt her breath quicken. It was her father. And so it was alone that the two met and for a fraction of a minute they stopped and stared at each other. Esther saw a man who did indeed resemble her father, but his hair was grey and the lines on his face had softened until she scarcely recognised the hard governor of her childhood. The father saw a child he would not have known: a tall, slender young woman, whose beauty shone through all the dust of travel and the deeper scars left by the life she had lived. He had heard some of her story from Joseph and had guessed the rest: he knew of the years of toil and poverty, suffering and degradation, and he knew too that he had driven her to this; his hand had laid on her the stamp of prostitute and slave, because he had failed to recognise the budding of a sweeter thing than either of them had known then, the yearning of a child of God to follow her true Master. It was this that was uppermost in his mind when suddenly, oblivious of all those who were now drawing near, he knelt at her feet and kissed them:

"Forgive me, my daughter," he said quietly. "I have not been worthy of the name of father."

With an inarticulate cry, Esther stooped to raise him and, with tears streaming down her face, she flung herself into his ready arms.

They were all around her now. Her mother, older but with a new happiness and confidence in her face, pressing close behind her husband to take Esther in her turn to her heart: Tara, miraculously tall and self-assured: and many, many more new friends surrounding her on every side. And so Esther came home.

*

I HAD MISSED THE FIRST SIX WEEKS of the new school year, so when I was asked to take reading in the first form because another teacher was ill, the girls were new to me. With the Principal, I watched the first-form girls go into their class-room. One girl particularly interested me.

"Who is that?" I asked the Principal, indicating the girl I meant.

"Her name is Esther," answered the Principal. "She entered school this year, supported in part by her parents and in part by the man she is going to marry. He is one of our colporteurs."

I studied the girl's face. It was radiant with happiness.

"Is she then already a Christian?" I asked.

"She gave as clear a testimony to the Lord's guidance and help as I have ever heard from a first-year student, last week," answered the Principal.

"And she cannot read?" I wondered.

"Not yet," was the answer. "Though I think she will before long. I hardly ever see her with the reading book out of her hand. But see for yourself. She is one of your pupils and the class is waiting."

I went in and tried to hide my interest in the girl by calling others to read before her. When it was her turn she read the required passage from St Luke with hardly a mistake. I found it hard to take my eyes from her intent and yet joyful face.

"You are doing very well," I told her and she smiled shyly.

"You see I have desired to learn for such a long time," she said softly, "and the Lord has only now enabled me to."

"Have you known the Lord long?" I asked, though that is not a usual question to a first termer.

"For many years," she said at once, and those wonderful eyes shone with a quiet happiness. Obviously she was just longing to tell me of her beloved Lord.

How had she learned of Him, I wondered? What kind of life had she had to make her trust in Him so much? Lines of sadness and hardship were on her face as well as of joy. A girl of this age, with this beauty, had not come straight from her mother's home. I realised she had turned the page and started to read again, and automatically began to follow the words with my pencil. Yes, I could read and teach such a girl to read. I could place in her hands, as had been placed in mine, the treasures of the knowledge of His Word. But what, I wondered, could she teach me of real suffering and hardship and how it can be endured; of patience in trouble; of finding Him sufficient in heart-breaking loneliness; or of eagerness, written in the very bend of her head over the book, to seek after Him and learn of Him?

I followed the lines that she was hesitatingly reading:

"*And Jesus came and said to them, All authority in heaven and on earth has been given to me. Go therefore and make disciples of all nations, baptising them in the name of the Father and of the Son and of the Holy Spirit, teaching them to observe all that I have commanded you; and lo, I am with you always, even unto the end of the world.*"